Praise for *Joan Garry's Guide to Nonprofit Leadership*

"WOW! I giggled, I pondered, I smiled, I nodded! Awesome! I share Joan's belief that nonprofits can change the world and she has given us the book that will make that happen! What's more, thanks to the way it is written, we'll be smiling as we learn!"

—Caryl Stern, President & CEO, U.S. Fund for UNICEF

"Joan has written a powerful, must-read book for nonprofit leaders. Her experience and compassion will motivate you in your journey to 'experiment your way to success.' Filled with good humor and free of jargon, this book provides readers with valuable lessons from one of the country's most skilled leadership coaches."

—Vikki Spruill, President & CEO, Council on Foundations

"As an instructor here at The Annenberg School, Joan has proven herself to be a joyful and inspiring educator, igniting student interest in the power of nonprofit communications. How fitting that she has invested time in sharing that joy and inspiration in *Joan Garry's Guide to Nonprofit Leadership*. Among the qualities that make for an effective nonprofit leader, writes Joan, are boldness, joy, a good sense of humor, and the ability to tell a good story. Not coincidentally, these same attributes describe her book perfectly. The arguments and advice are bold and illustrated by a range of engaging and personal stories drawn from her career as one of the nation's most influential nonprofit leaders."

—Michael X. Delli Carpini, Dean, The Annenberg School for Communication, University of Pennsylvania

"Joan understands nonprofits the way a great mechanic understands cars—from years of getting her hands dirty under the hood. *Joan Garry's Guide to Nonprofit Leadership* is the owner's manual nonprofit leaders need. Her take is always serious, but never solemn; right but not self-righteous. She's the wise friend every nonprofit leader needs. I know I do."
    —**Rabbi Rick Jacobs, President, Union for Reform Judaism**

"As an overworked nonprofit ED with one eye twitching due to cash-flow issues, I am always skeptical of people claiming to be 'experts' about nonprofit leadership. Joan, however, proves to be not only an authority on our work, but also no-nonsense, down-to-earth, and hilarious. This book is chock-full of helpful stories and concrete recommendations, delivered in Joan's usual engaging conversational tone, sprinkled with jokes and witticisms. You feel like you're venting with a wise and caring friend at happy hour. There is great advice here for new as well as experienced nonprofit leaders."
    —**Vu Le, Blogger, Nonprofit with Balls**

"While it may sound idiotic to think about curling up with a good book on management and leadership, that's how great this book is. *Joan Garry's Guide to Nonprofit Leadership* is brilliant, practical, beautifully written, hysterically funny, insightful, moving, entertaining, original, incredibly useful, emotionally satisfying, and right about just about everything. There's something useful and enjoyable on every page, and there is no excuse for not buying it immediately."
    —**Kenneth Cloke, Author, *Resolving Conflicts at Work* and *The End of Management and the Rise of Organizational Democracy***

JOAN GARRY'S
GUIDE TO
Nonprofit
Leadership

Because Nonprofits are Messy

JOAN GARRY

WILEY

Published by John Wiley & Sons, Inc., Hoboken, New Jersey.
Published simultaneously in Canada.

Chapter cartoons: Marcel Hirschegger/Abstract Edge, www.abstractedge.com.

For general information about our other products and services, please contact our Customer Care Department within the United States at (800) 762-2974, outside the United States at (317) 572-3993 or fax (317) 572-4002.

Wiley publishes in a variety of print and electronic formats and by print-on-demand. Some material included with standard print versions of this book may not be included in e-books or in print-on-demand. If this book refers to media such as a CD or DVD that is not included in the version you purchased, you may download this material at http://booksupport.wiley.com. For more information about Wiley products, visit www.wiley.com.

Library of Congress Cataloging-in-Publication Data:

Names: Garry, Joan, author.
Title: Joan Garry's guide to nonprofit leadership : because nonprofits are messy /
   Joan Garry.
Description: Hoboken, New Jersey : John Wiley & Sons, Inc., [2017] | Includes
   bibliographical references and index.
Identifiers: LCCN 2016055627 (print) | LCCN 2017006905 (ebook) |
   ISBN 9781119293064 (cloth) | ISBN 9781119293095 (pdf) |
   ISBN 9781119293101 (epub)
Subjects: LCSH: Nonprofit organizations–Management. | Boards of directors. |
   Leadership.
Classification: LCC HD62.6 .G36 2017 (print) | LCC HD62.6 (ebook) |
   DDC 658.4/092–dc23
LC record available at https://lccn.loc.gov/2016055627

Printed in the United States of America.

10 9 8 7 6 5 4 3 2

Contents

Acknowledgments

We are who we are because of the families that raised us. My mom passed away just after I completed this manuscript. As we went through her purse, I found a copy of the cover art for the book. On an otherwise dreary day, it made me smile. Until her last day, my mom was sharp as a tack. If I am smart, feisty, funny, and a bit of a dog with a bone about issues that feel important to me, it is because I am my mother's daughter. To steal a line from one of my kids, *Thanks for birthing me, Mom.*

My dad taught me the power of being a good coach. I saw him in action during years of being his right hand in Little League dugouts. And I admired him. Offering direction, support, and encouragement, he was not just a coach. He was a champion, and an educator. A quiet leader. Everyone wanted to be on his team. I was lucky. I was born into his team.

Father Jim Loughran, SJ, of blessed memory, taught my first philosophy class. He challenged me to consider the value of my moral compass, my own intellectual capacity and the power of inquiry.

We are who we are because of the people who shape our thinking during our journey. Attorneys Paula Ettelbrick and Suzanne Goldberg represented our family in a precedent-setting case to create a legal connection between our kids and me. These two triggered the activist in me, planting the idea in my head that it was time to get off the sidelines and onto the field.

In 1985, Showtime engaged consultants Joan Goldsmith and Ken Cloke. Joan and Ken were evangelists about making teamwork a reality (not a buzzword) in workplaces. And they taught me about the power of difficult conversations. Much of my work today feels like the baton they passed on to me.

Yes, this was the village that led me from a solid happy life to a life with real purpose—leading me to the nonprofit sector and never looking back.

During my tenure at GLAAD, I met activists, donors, and volunteers who inspired me to do my best for them. Lessons learned from this journey are too long to list but special thanks to "heart monitor Julie" and the five-star staff and board who partnered with me to build an organization to last. I hope you are lucky enough to find someone like Karen Magee to step into a board leadership role. I can talk about the power of that partnership because I speak from experience with Karen.

This book presents my chance to reach more people with guidance and direction. My deepest thanks to Scott Paley of Abstract Edge for believing that I had something to say and for working tirelessly to ensure that my message reaches far and wide. Without a blog and a podcast (both Scott's idea), there would be no book.

Seth Rosen, a coaching client from years ago and now the senior member of my team, was the first person to utter the words "So, when are you gonna write a book?" Thank you, Seth, for planting the seed and recognizing that leaders need authentic, compassionate, and practical advice with a dose of good humor added for good measure. As my right hand, Debbie McNally is great with clients, a first-rate writer and editor and often makes that one comment in a meeting that brings the conversation into especially clear focus.

Special thanks to my best friend since age 14, Kim Freedman. Through this process, as she has through life, Kim has been a cheerleader, a fierce advocate for my brand, and a first-rate thought partner from Day One to put my passion into print.

Thank you so much to Arielle Eckstut, my "book doctor," and Jim Levine, my agent at Levine Greenberg Rostan Literary Agency. Jim was a nonprofit leader in a former life and I could not have asked for a better advocate who really understands that nonprofits are messy. And of course I am so grateful to my friends and colleagues at John Wiley & Sons for believing in me (and for agreeing to put an image of a garbage can on the cover of one of their books).

Lastly, we are who we are because of the families we create. I never thought I'd be so lucky to have one and try never to take it for granted. I keep a Chinese fortune cookie note in my desk drawer. It reads simply: *You Have A Colorful Family*. Amen. Thanks to my three kids, Scout, Ben, and Kit, for letting me catch you, raise you, annoy you, amuse you, and love you with all my heart.

And, of course, to my legal wife of 3 years and spouse for 35, Eileen Opatut. In 1996, she casually suggested I leave the for-profit sector and apply for a nonprofit executive director job. We had three kids under seven and had just bought a big house: perfect time for a new low-paying job. She saw, as she always does, what I often miss completely—I was a leader and an advocate ready for a cause.

And so began a new chapter in my life. A life that turned from black and white to color the day we met. Like Dorothy's arrival to Oz. Complete with three munchkins.

"Of course you're tired. Changing the world is an exhausting business."

Introduction

I could have killed my development director.

And I don't mean it the way you think.

Julie arrived at a quarterly board meeting. She didn't look quite right. It was hard not to notice that there was something protruding from her blouse.

A heart monitor.

She had flown from Los Angeles to Chicago and I had flown in from New York. We had not seen each other in a few weeks.

Maybe she mentioned something about a doctor's appointment, but come on. I was leading a nonprofit trying to save a portion of the world. Who has time for the health and well-being of staff?

Clearly not me.

I'm sure you're wondering. Julie is fine. Today, she is a clinical psychologist who no doubt helps clients contend with Type A, oblivious bosses who drive their employees to heart problems.

Oh, also, in case you are wondering, the board meeting was a big hit. Julie and I were impressive and on our game—as we usually were. I did get a few comments at the breaks, like "Hey, how's Julie?" or "Julie looks like the job is taking a toll on her." "No worries," I said. And went on to get an A+ on our board meeting presentation.

But wow. *Who was I?* Why did I not tell Julie to turn on her heels and take the next flight home to Los Angeles?

I am not insane. I swear. I would never intentionally try to put Julie (or anyone else for that matter) in harm's way.

But nonprofits can cause a person to transform into someone they don't recognize.

Why?

Because nonprofits are messy.

It's inherent in the formula of the unique beast we call a 501(c)(3).

$$A + B + C + a \text{ big dose of intense passion} = MESSY$$

A. A poorly paid and overworked group (staff) that . . .
B. Relies on the efforts of people who get paid nothing (volunteers) and are overseen by . . .
C. Another group of volunteers who get paid nothing and are supposed to give and get lots of money (board)

All of this is in the service of something that every single one of them cares passionately about. Wow. Now that is a recipe for messy. And that organization you care so deeply about can get messier still if not led and managed well.

I learned the messy lesson the hard way.

What did I know? Fifteen years in corporate America and then *poof*! I'm running a nonprofit (more on the "poof" part in a few).

I felt ever so well equipped with my financial skills, my management skills, and my understanding of how to manage a budget and to deliver results.

I had never met "messy" like this until the day I sat down at my desk at GLAAD (formerly, the Gay and Lesbian Alliance Against Defamation and now just the acronym), one of the largest gay rights nonprofit organizations. Or so I thought.

It actually was large by reputation but "large" was not the first word that came to mind when I saw that we had only $360 in the bank. *Large* was not at all the word that came to mind.

It was really bad. And I'll admit it here—I felt like a bit of a fraud, soon to be unmasked as having neither the grit nor the skills to dig us out.

There was one very bad day the first week on the job. I remember it well.

I was at my computer, writing a solicitation letter to a lapsed donor—trying *everything* to drive cash in the door. I was pleased with the letter. I sent it to print on the serviceable printer, reviewed it, and found a typo.

And with that I burst into tears. It may have been my predicament but I think it was singularly focused. I knew we could not afford to reorder another letterhead.

Then there was this other day.

I was in Los Angeles meeting with donors (and praying they would pick up the tab) when my phone rang. It was my deputy director in New York. He calmly said that it might be time to look for office space he knew we couldn't afford.

There was an inch of snow on his desk when he arrived for work.

Very, very messy.

I'm not sure I knew what to expect when I left corporate America for this job. I'm not sure I did a lot of thinking. My move from the corporate world to the nonprofit world was more of a "heart" move than a "head" move.

* * *

I was not unhappy in the corporate world. Hardly. I had hit the corporate jackpot. In my first job out of college, I landed on the management team of MTV.

Yes, working at MTV in the early 1980s was just as cool as you can imagine. I also learned a ton. I learned about the pace, intensity, and thrill of being a part of a start-up (more on that later). I learned how to innovate when I wrote the business plan for the MTV Video Music Awards. And my Harvard MBA boss bought me an HP12c calculator (the calculator that allows people to *assume* you have an MBA) and taught me about budgets and balance sheets.

From MTV, I moved to Showtime Networks. There, I became a very good manager of people. I became a team player. I learned what it meant to be a good corporate citizen as one of the early gay poster children when Showtime began to walk the walk on diversity. We gave money to worthy causes and I found myself in the early 1990s advocating for corporate sponsorship dollars from Showtime to gay organizations.

While I was there, we built a new business, a now-dinosaur that we called pay-per-view. And it was there that I learned about boxing.

Yes, boxing. Like that thing big, sweaty guys do with gloves on in rings.

I learned that people pay a lot of money to watch boxing on TV. And that if you get really good seats at the MGM Grand Hotel in Las Vegas, the flying sweat . . . well, it flies.

The most important gift Showtime gave me was the recognition that I had a voice. I became another kind of poster child—essentially an employee advocate for better communication and transparency from the senior leadership. This work, which included hosting a full-staff (800) town meeting, was transformative.

I found my voice as an *advocate* for the employees at Showtime.

I found my wheelhouse.

Now what? I had no idea. I just knew a change was in the offing.

There was no "aha" moment for me. There was just a conversation. Eileen, my now wife but then spouse, partner, longtime companion, (enter other euphemisms here) came home from work and told me that the executive director job at GLAAD was open.

I casually remarked, "You know, somebody like me ought to have a job like that. We have three kids, I drive a minivan, and we really do have a white picket fence. That would shake up America's picture of a gay-rights activist, huh?"

Eileen, who knows how to shake things up in just the right way, casually responded to my casual remark. "Well then, somebody like you should apply."

I never in a million years thought they would hire me. No nonprofit experience and I had never asked a soul for money before.

But they hired somebody like me. A lot like me. So me it was me. As my good friend Amy says, "Well, slap my fanny!"

I guess I should have asked more questions before I took the job. That said, it probably would not have mattered. The board didn't have the answers either. The GLAAD *brand* may have been big but the problems were way bigger. I impressed myself with a tough salary negotiation that proved meaningless because all they could afford to pay me was $360. But just a one-time payment. That was the sum total in the GLAAD bank account.

How did I manage? Well, nobody handed me a book—that's for sure. I don't even remember anyone telling me that everything was going to be okay. It was *my* job to tell everyone *else* that everything was going to be okay.

There was so much I didn't know. Like *everything,* it seemed.

I wish there *had* been a book—one with practical advice about how to untangle all of this mess written by someone who had stood in my shoes. Written by someone who would be my advocate, help me realize that I was not alone and maybe even make me laugh about sobbing over a piece of stationery.

So I decided to write the book I wish someone had handed me.

Because my experience as a nonprofit leader and then a board member and major donor and today the principal in a nonprofit consulting practice has taught me a great deal that I believe will help you as a nonprofit leader become more effective at your jobs and remind you of the joy you can find in being underpaid and overworked to save even the smallest part of the world.

Maybe you are wondering how I untangled the knots at GLAAD without a book.☺

We did indeed dig it out. I left the organization eight years later with a $1.5 million cash reserve, an $8 million budget, and a staff of over 40. But that's not what counts.

We made an impact. Long before marriage equality, GLAAD put same sex couples on the wedding pages of every major newspaper in America. Starting with the *New York Times.*

If you think there are too many gay characters on television, give it to me right between the eyes. Our work at GLAAD brought us there. If the name Matthew Shepard, the young gay man murdered in Wyoming in 1998, is familiar to you, it's because GLAAD shaped that into a national story, ensuring that any discussion about hate crimes expanded to include sexual orientation. A lasting legacy for a young man from Laramie.

How did we do it?

The recipe is not unique to my leadership or to GLAAD. There are universal constants.

Between my own personal experience and working with hundreds of board and nonprofit staff leaders, these constants are critical to either digging out, stabilizing, or taking your organization to a place of even greater impact.

You need to rely on the strengths and power of those around you and see your varying stakeholder groups as a village, each with a very important role to play in the success of your organization.

Then there is the mission. Your passion for it and your ability to articulate it, why it's important, and what impact it is having on the world. (I continue to be stunned by how infrequently leaders get this right.) You have to cultivate your storytelling skills and in so doing, you will cultivate your fundraising prowess.

Recognize the skills and attributes of your staff and manage them with compassion and accountability (now *that* is a delicate balance). You have to be transparent and authentic with both successes and challenges. Recognize that you are slightly more like a tribe than a staff.

See the board as a resource and invest time and energy in building a committed and diverse group. Be an active member of the board recruitment committee from Day One. And seek out strong co-chairs and consider them partners. Avoid the "yes" folks. Strong chairs will give you great advice and ask tough questions. Try not to get defensive and this pushback will make you a more effective leader.

Once your organization stops teetering (see the preceding steps), budget money annually to build a reserve. Once you are able to pull your nose out of the cash flow worksheet, you can actually think ahead. So get to it. Where are the gaps? Are there constituents you are not serving that no other organization can serve as well as you? These conversations can lead to smart and bold strategies and fundable plans for the future.

This is how to dig out, how to stabilize, how to thrive. This is the core of my advice to many of my clients, to the thousands who visit my blog weekly and to the dozens who write weekly with questions. And this captures the spirit of the advice I hope will be valuable to you.

> The single most important attribute of a nonprofit leader—board member or staff leader—the attribute that is most critical in helping you to untangle knots and the one that can move your organization from good to great—is joy.

But the single most important attribute of a nonprofit leader—board member or staff leader—the attribute that is most critical in helping you to untangle knots and the one that can move your organization from good to great—is joy.

In my own experience as a staff leader and a board leader along with work with all of the clients I have had through the years, it is this attribute that creates standout leaders. They get it. It is a joy to be paid to advocate, feed the hungry, to change laws, to raise money, to create a strong infrastructure—all in the service of others.

*   *   *

I believe deeply in the power of the nonprofit sector to change the world. In ways large and small. If you have raised your hand to say, "I want to help. I want to work here. I want to volunteer. I want to raise money for you," you are, in my book, *nobility*.

Your work says something important about your character, your spirit, your commitment to a fair and just world, your integrity, your courage, your grit and perseverance.

Not everyone makes this choice. Far too many people with time, connections, and capacity sit on the sidelines.

You made a different choice.

Your feet are firmly planted on the high road. And know that you are admired.

By many. Including me.

I speak from experience. Traveling on the high road isn't easy and it's messy but if you love your organization, it's worth every minute.

Nonprofits are messy. Not enough money. Too many cooks. An overdose of passion.

Leading nonprofits isn't easy.

I'm here to help.

"You want to use x-ray vision to spy on an Executive Session meeting? No, I don't think that's a great idea."

Chapter 1 The Superpowers of Nonprofit Leadership

Dear Joan:

I've been with my organization for nearly eight years, most recently in a development role. My predecessor has been the voice and face of the organization for nearly 25 years and has just retired. The board has offered me the E.D. position.

This would be alien territory for me. I've been the relationship guy and I keep the trains running on time.

And the truth is I'm not exactly sure what I would be getting into. I want to give this a go but I think I need help and would like to retain you as a coach.

My goal is simple: I want to learn to behave like an executive director.

Signed,
E.D. "E.T."

"To behave like an executive director." A very good goal for an executive director, I might add.

E.T. became a client and we teased out exactly what he meant by this.

To be a leader and not a department head. To worry about the whole organization and every stakeholder. To stare at cash flow and wonder about payroll. To take responsibility for partnering with the board so that its members can fulfill their obligations. To stand up at a gala and give an inspiring and motivating speech. To feel an overwhelming sense of responsibility for the communities you serve.

It's a hard role and a hard role to cast for. I am currently working with a board that cannot agree on the role the executive director should play (and they are already interviewing candidates!). (Can *you* say, "Cart before the horse"?)

Who should a board be looking for? What matters? In small organizations, the staff leader really *does* do it all. A person who can inspire a group with her words *and* read a balance sheet? What skills and attributes matter? Do you have them? How do you cultivate them?

And the decision is so important. In my experience, leadership transitions are *the* most destabilizing forces in a nonprofit organization. Try raising money when you are between executive directors. 'Nuff said.

What's interesting is that all these same issues and questions apply to board chairs as well. What should an organization be looking for in a board chair? (Note: the correct answer is *not* "Pray that someone raises her hand and pick her.") How might the skills and attributes of that person complement those of the staff leader? What skills and attributes matter? How do you cultivate them?

A QUIZ

Before I give you the answer to these questions, let's try a little quiz. Are you currently a nonprofit E.D., overwhelmed by the idea that you need to be all things to all people? A board chair enthusiastic about leading the board to support the staff? Or someone who aspires to change the world and make the for-profit to nonprofit leap?

The quiz should put things into perspective and begin to reveal the superpowers.

So riddle me this, Batmen and -women, it's time to pick your next board chair or executive director. Here are the finalists:

- Superman
- Spiderman
- Gumby
- Kermit the Frog

Let's dissect this, shall we? (Oh, apologies to Kermit—not a good word for frogs.)

Each of these four have amazing strengths. Perhaps at first blush, you figure any of them could be a five-star nonprofit leader.

Superman?

This guy has some serious things going for him:

- Sometimes organizations just want someone to swoop in and save the day.
- He's dripping with integrity and tells the truth.
- He is very smart.
- Would you say, "No" to him if he asked you for a donation?
- He has a fabulous outfit (I hear capes might be coming back).

Spiderman?

Lots of appeal here, too. He's human, powerful, and nerdy. He's vulnerable but strong. Some comic book fanatics say he is the single greatest superhero of them all.

- He has real humanity—vulnerabilities, guilt, and flaws.
- He's driven. Peter Parker, the man behind Spiderman, helps people because he understands the price of not doing it—he could have prevented his uncle's death.
- He grows into his power. The responsibility of leadership is not something he asks for but he accepts it and uses that responsibility to the best of his ability.

Gumby?

One of my senior staff members gave me a small Gumby figure I have right here on my desk. When I look at him, I am reminded that not everything is black and white and that being flexible is absolutely key to success in any setting. Is Gumby your man?

- He's well rounded.
- Very optimistic—would lead with an optimism that his organization could change the world.
- He's someone you want to be around—kind, warm-hearted, and generous.
- He has real humanity—vulnerabilities, guilt, and flaws.

Kermit?

Another guy with some solid skills and attributes for nonprofit leadership:

- A team builder. He can bring a diverse group together. Anyone who can get Gonzo, Fozzie, and Miss Piggy working toward a common goal has a real superpower.
- Kermit is an optimist but not a Pollyanna. He can get down sometimes too, but in the end, he has a vision and rallies the Muppets around it.
- He cares deeply about doing the right thing.
- Kermit is your go-to guy in a crisis.
- Strong planning skills.
- His ego is just the right size—he can and does admit mistakes.

Time to put the four of them to the test. Here's the kind of situation each of them may encounter. Then you get to make your choice.

You need a new board chair. The previous leader didn't want the job—might have been in the restroom during elections. Committees are dormant. The board does a decent job selling tickets to your big gala but half of them don't want to pay for a ticket themselves. The founder of the organization is a big personality and when she stepped down two years ago, she offered to join the board and your previous board chair couldn't say no. She isn't letting go of the job. Your E.D. is a good performer but the founder is driving her mad. You are worried she may be recruited away.

Who is the guy for the job? (I just grabbed a few superhero prototypes—there are lots of great women leaders out there, too.)

Superman is the command-and-control nonprofit leader. The world is quite black and white for him. He would see board members as "good guys" or "bad guys." We know the world is not that simple. Nonprofit leadership demands both an understanding and an *appreciation* for *nuance* and the land of the *gray*. We know this type. A good leader to dig you out fast, but not the marathon guy.

Spiderman is a more empathetic, three-dimensional leader. His downfall is the challenge of many leaders—*insecurity*.

Gumby? What a nice guy. Who would not want to sit and hear about an organization from somebody like Gumby? He is a relationship builder of the highest order. But his fatal leadership flaw? He is a pleaser. Now most nonprofit leaders have some pleaser stuff going on. But if it drives you, you are done for. You have various stakeholders and pleasing everyone usually means pleasing no one. And your job isn't about pleasing. It's about serving your mission.

Okay. So I've given the answer away.

My vote goes to Kermit, hands down.

First off, Kermit would have figured out some way to give the founder a big role with no real power. Look how he manages Piggy. He would rally the troops without shaming them. He would find the key strength in each board member and bring out the best in each of them. He would not be overly bossy with the E.D.—he'd offer his support and be more like a coach. And he would help staff and board keep their eyes on the prize, never losing sight of the organization's mission and vision.

Kermit may not thrive in a hierarchical work environment but he'd be a rock star E.D. or board chair.

Kermit is not perfect and he knows it. But so key to effective leadership, it makes him a good delegator! He is all about the team and he understands the value each brings to the work. He believes in diversity. He likes to work to reach consensus but never loses sight of the end game—he is always true to the cause. He is fair and listens and he can manage high-maintenance personalities without sacrificing the work. I also think he can disagree and his team ultimately listens and respects the decision (the decision they feel was made with their input).

He understands what it takes to be a great leader in the nonprofit sector.

He understands that power comes from all around you.

He recognizes that developing core leadership *attributes* is as important as skills building.

YOU'RE NOT ON TOP OF ANYTHING

In 1997, the Coors Brewing Company approached me, as the executive director of GLAAD. They were interested in making a $50,000 corporate sponsorship donation to our organization. As our organization was still on a financial respirator, I was interested. Very interested.

But I knew the history of Coors and the gay community—the Coors family had deep ties to the Heritage Foundation, a significant funder of organizations leading the opposition to LGBT equality. As a result, there had been a longstanding boycott in the gay community. Drink any beer you like but not Coors.

A discussion with Coors illustrated to me that the company was better on gay issues inside its organization (domestic partner benefits and other nondiscrimination policies) than many other companies that supported GLAAD.

Should I accept the sponsorship money and in so doing help rebuild the Coors brand in the gay community? The decision was mine to make.

Or was it?

In Jim Collins's monograph *From Good to Great in the Social Sector,* he makes the case that power and decision making in the nonprofit sector is different from (and messier than) how it is in the private sector.

To be a great leader, you must erase your preconceived notions of what it means to be in charge, and this starts with a standard organizational chart (see Figure 1.1).

FIGURE 1.1   The basic org chart we all know and understand.

POWER AND AUTHORITY

You probably have a piece of paper that shows this kind of hierarchy. Time to recycle.

Is it factually accurate? Yup. Is it how you should look at or exert your power as a nonprofit leader? Absolutely not.

Now take a look at the chart shown in Figure 1.2.

Using the org chart in Figure 1.1, the Coors decision is easy. I make a statement about the changes at Coors, accept the donation, make payroll, and let the chips fall where they may.

In the nonprofit sector, a leader is beholden to vast and diverse stakeholders. I was hired to run GLAAD in the service of moving the needle forward on equal rights for the community I served. The bottom line matters, of course, but only to ensure that you have sufficient resources to work in the service of your mission.

In the org chart in Figure 1.2, the executive director derives power from all around her. This is why former Girl Scout E.D. Frances Hesselbein once told a reporter that she saw herself in the center and that she "was not on top of anything."

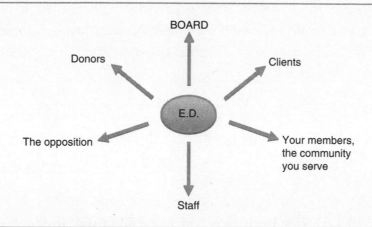

FIGURE 1.2 Picture it this way instead. The power comes from around you.

So what did this mean for the Coors decision? The voices of the stakeholder groups around me were critical. I needed to be well informed, I needed strong input from different groups, and I needed a thought partner in my board chair to kick around the pros and cons. I knew the decision was ultimately mine but I never really thought of it that way. We were all in this together.

My development director (the one I nearly killed—see the intro) was outraged and feared we would lose more money than we earned by accepting Coors' donation. We did our due diligence and determined that would not be the case. The staff was mixed—some worried I would be eaten alive by the press (given my own corporate background) either way; others thought rejecting the money could be unfair to Coors when in fact, by corporate standards, they were leaders on gay issues.

This kind of power demands that you meet with the leaders of the Coors Boycott Committee—not to empower them but to ensure their voices are heard. We even invited them to a board meeting.

And this kind of power demands that you see the decision from all sides. We secured a meeting with the most senior people at Coors and garnered commitments from them to do more than just donate money.

And this kind of power demanded that I put myself at a national LGBT conference in which several hundred community members could share their distaste with the thought that GLAAD may make this choice. In this setting, you can be sure that I heard them. Many of them were yelling at me.

In the end, Coors became a corporate sponsor of GLAAD. Not everyone agreed but everyone had a voice. All stakeholder groups were heard and our entire process and strategy was smarter and more effective than any decision I had made on my own. This is what Jim Collins means when he talks about power in the nonprofit sector being "diffuse." And at its best, it creates a staff that feels valued and heard, a supportive board comfortable with challenging, and a membership that sees a process rich with integrity.

So you can see how this can get messy, right? How quickly a staff can become entitled. The same goes for your clients. You want them to be engaged in the work, but to secure their opinions about decisions and policies, you must walk a fine line. If you don't, you wind up with entitled stakeholders and you wind up fighting to make decisions that are in the best interest of the entire organization.

Consider a board chair who has already made up his or her mind about the E.D. annual review process and doesn't ask for input. How valuable does the full board feel? I'm going to go with "not very." Or how about an E.D. who has already made a big decision and asks the senior staff to weigh in? That E.D. better pray the senior staff comes up with the same decision. Then, there is the E.D. who listens to input and finds herself more indecisive than when she first asked.

Each of these scenarios makes things messier.

WHAT DO I *DO* WITH ALL THIS?

Not everyone is Kermit. And no one fits neatly into one of these four profiles. You might identify with someone outside the list (hoping there are no Darth Vaders among you).

The key is to recognize attributes that don't serve you well, and make adjustments. So for me, I think I am an "SK"—a Superman–Kermit combo. (Yes, I am now making fun of every personality profile test you've ever been subjected to at work or during a retreat.)

I am a fixer. I know this about myself. I love to save the day—that's why I love my work—I have serious Superman tendencies. They serve me well in my business, but as a nonprofit leader, not so much. I like to think I have some Kermit going on as well. Like Kermit, I like to think of myself as an orchestra conductor, bringing out the best in my tribe.

So what if you're not like Kermit?

Superman Tendencies

Thomas arrived as the new E.D. of a pretty small organization—budget size a few hundred thousand. Thomas wears a cape and not just on Halloween. He arrived at his organization to fix it; to save the day. The organization had been in disarray for some time.

Thomas started weekly staff meetings and no one came. Well, some did but most didn't. They were too busy. Thomas was angry and he threatened consequences. The following week, attendance was better, but still not great. Attitudes were even worse.

What was he missing?

Thomas made several incorrect assumptions:

- *If you tell people what to do, they will just do it.* Now that worked like a charm for me in Catholic grammar school in the

1960s, but in a nonprofit, you really need your staff to feel some sense of ownership of the decisions made. This is what they deserve in lieu of that year-end bonus that is coming like NEVER.

- *He assumed they understood*—in this case, he assumed they understood the value of a staff meeting. That's not how the previous leader managed (or didn't).

So here are the changes I suggested that he make:

- *Have a meeting about the meeting.* Send an email around. Tell folks that this meeting is to talk about how a staff meeting might be valuable to the entire group and to each staffer. Let them figure out the need themselves. And yes, everyone showed up. They built a standing agenda that was more than just reporting out, and staff meetings are now weekly and well attended.

- *Ask more questions.* Cape-wearers are fixers and they know the answers. Maybe they are arrogant or maybe just very self-assured. Thomas liked to just tell staff the answers, and direct them closely because he was clear about what needed to be done. I encouraged Thomas to ask staff members what *they* would do. Have a conversation about strategy. Guide *gently* if they are off base, and more importantly, *listen carefully.* You know, it is possible that *they are right* and you are not (I know—hard to believe).

- *Dip your toe into the world of the "gray."* To Superman, things are black or white. There are good guys and bad guys. Things need to happen a *certain* way. You need to *try* to appreciate the gray. This might mean you have to own the fact that you are not as open-minded as you need to be. Are you a board chair ready to write off a board member who does nothing? Try having a coffee with said board member. Ask her what success looks like for her, what she needs from the chair to be successful. Don't vote her off the island too quickly. Move from black to gray.

Spiderman Tendencies

Unlike Clark Kent, who is clearly "pretending," Peter Parker is a 3-dimensional teenager—a nerd, an introvert, and an outsider. A sensitive soul who has experienced tragedy and loss. Spidey, on the other hand, owns his brilliance and is all about victory, but both Peter and Spidey share two key things—(1) the importance of the intersection of knowledge and power, and (2) a core value to lead a responsible life.

Kim began her job as a board chair, deeply insecure about her ability to do a good job (get in line, Kim). She was now in charge of a sizable board filled with some very high-powered folks. If you spent an hour with this group and someone asked you who the chair was, she would not be your obvious first guess. Kim was not a great public speaker and was intimidated by the resumes of those folks around the table, none of whom, by the way, were willing to step into the leadership role. But Kim knew the board needed someone dedicated, someone who loved the organization and really wanted the staff leader to succeed.

Kim's challenge was to not be overrun by the bombastic folks in the room—to establish leadership. But Kim doesn't wear a cape.

In our coaching sessions, Kim and I spoke about where her power comes from. I learned that she was deeply empathetic and had a profound and personal connection to the mission. I also learned that she was smart as hell.

The following shifts helped Kim quite a bit.

- *Be the most knowledgeable person in the room.* I'm not talking about smarts. I'm talking about the professional aspects of the role of board chair. I begged her to buy *Robert's Rules of Order*. It is amazing how much respect a board chair can garner when managing a meeting professionally. I also encouraged her to spend time really understanding the nonprofit sector and the complexities and context of the issue the organization was up against.

- *Play to your strengths.* Remember Kim's empathy? Remember her introvert tendencies? We devised a regular email from the board chair. It opened with a story about the work or something Kim had learned about the broader context of the work, reminding board members why they serve. Then she was able to call board members to action. She had put the requests into an emotional and intellectual context.

Gumby Tendencies

Pleasers cause themselves heaps of trouble. Attempting to make everyone happy inevitably backfires in nearly every situation—from a kindergarten class to a boardroom to a staff meeting.

The most important lesson I have learned about Gumby leaders is that if you can help them draw a picture of what happens as a result of pleasing, it makes them really unhappy. Gumbys respond in the moment and do not anticipate well. It's kind of like an automatic camera—"point and shoot." Trouble to the left? Let me fix it. Conflicting trouble to the right? I'll make you happy, too. But they can't look far enough down the road to see the implications.

Tina is an E.D. of a direct service organization that has a very strong client advocacy group. There had long been a push to put a member of that group on the board. Attempting to please the Client Advocacy Task Force, the E.D. brought the group into a board meeting to talk about it so the group could make the pitch. Then it was time to please the board. They loved the idea.

Meanwhile Ben, director of programs, saw the challenge from a mile away. He could see that electing the chair of the task force to the board could give that task force undue power. He saw that it would be very difficult for this person to be anything other than a representative of the task force rather than someone who could view the organization from 35,000 feet—like an effective board member must.

The outcome was not pleasing. The new board member came to advocate for clients. In and of itself, this was okay but an idea he brought to the table was not in the best interest of the organization, and the board voted it down. He quit the board and undermined the credibility and reputation of the E.D. with anyone who would listen, including fellow board members. The E.D., displeased with how she was being treated, was recruited away. A messy leadership transition ensued (more on that in Chapter 8).

Some advice for the pleasers out there.

1. *Tell your board chair (partner) that you have a bit of a blind spot.* Gasp! Am I really suggesting that you tell your board chair that you are imperfect? Yup! You are partners, remember? Ask your board chair to help you think through the implications of decisions because you need help exercising your anticipation muscle.
2. *Remember that a pleaser moves too quickly and consciously slow yourself down.* The word "yes" can come out of your mouth *so* fast. Please count to 10 (or 20 or more) before saying anything. Even better, practice these words: *"Let me go back to my team and talk about this. They will have an important perspective on this issue."*
3. *Keep your eye on the mission at all times.* If you do, you will make better decisions and you will say, "No" when you need to. You will be more effective in the long run and that will be pleasing for everyone who cares about your mission.

4. *Bonus:* What not to do: *Do not look for a bad cop!* I have seen this too many times to count. A vice chair who leans into the board about their fundraising commitment. A deputy director who institutes tough new HR policies while the E.D. is out of town. This is unfair to the "bad cop" and a clear sign of an ineffective leader. If you can't put on your "big kid pants" and make tough decisions, please reevaluate your line of work.

WHAT WAS THIS QUIZ REALLY ABOUT?

Think about what we have been talking about here. Have I mentioned anything about specific fundraising prowess? How often your board should meet? How effectively your organization measures success? Or what role the audit committee should play in the development of the annual budget?

Nope. Those are skills. I wasn't talking about skills. I was talking about attributes. Because this is my pet peeve. Far too often, leaders are selected on the basis of skills. *"Well, David was the chair of the board of his alma mater—so he knows what the job is all about."* Does he? Does he have the right attributes to run a meeting and attempt to build consensus, or the discipline not to roll his eyes when a fellow board member says something awfully stupid?

Attributes matter as much, if not more than skills. Attributes. Or perhaps, given the roll we are on in this chapter, we should dub them "superpowers."

THE FIVE KEY SUPERPOWERS

Dear Joan,
I chair the E.D. search committee for our organization and we are in the final rounds with two very different

candidates. One is well known in our community and would bring gravitas to our organization. He is known to be a great fundraiser; finance and management skills are not his forte and his background in media (our sandbox) is slim. The other candidate is from corporate America, basically unknown in our sector, strong in our sandbox, known for strong management, and zero fundraising experience.

Oh, and did I mention that we may not hit payroll next week? And that we owe a quarter of a million dollars to vendors?

Whom should we hire . . . . Help!

Signed, Conflicted in the Boardroom

Trust me. Any search committee could have written this.

And it's not just a board dilemma.

It's universal to anyone inside or outside of an organization considering a move into leadership. Thinking about throwing your hat in the ring for a promotion at your school—you've been a teacher but never a fundraiser? Are you the COO who feels ready for the leadership gig? Are you a current board chair with no fundraising experience? Could you be an E.D. who won't admit to a soul that the balance sheet is total gibberish to you?

And it's a dilemma for current leaders, working to be the nonprofit leaders their organizations deserve.

A number of years ago, a statewide human rights organization had a similar dilemma. Hire the candidate with deep roots in the issue—well-known in the community, strong media skills, and a fundraising track record.

The other finalist—no chops in the sector. Not a fundraiser. Came from the labor movement. You know the movement where you need to get lots of people on the same page and then fight for what you believe in? A movement in which your reps have to trust you, allow you to lead—one in which relationship-building is key?

They picked the labor candidate. This candidate grabbed the reins and the organization grew in scope and impact in very short order.

How did this hire get made?

Someone on that search committee encouraged the group to consider the "chop-less" candidate through a different lens.

> Attributes may in fact be the true superpowers of leadership.

Through the lens of key leadership *attributes*. And in my opinion, attributes may in fact be the true superpowers of leadership.

And yes, I have a list.

• *Conviction:* As each of you knows, nonprofit leadership is no walk in the park. Hey, why should it be? You are moving mountains. But without conviction in the real promise of the organization, no one will follow your lead. When I coach clients who have been leaders for a long time, I often ask, *"Are you as passionate about the mission of this organization as you were when you arrived?"* When I hear a pause of any sort, we talk about it. A lot.

• *Authenticity:* Real leadership demands it. So too does fundraising. Because it is the foundational attribute of trust.

Ever been to a fundraiser when the head of the school, or board chair is talking to you but not looking at you and not listening to you? Rather, she is, but to spot the next donor on her list—you know, the one who gives more than you do. Icky right? Because there is nothing genuine about your interaction. I'm guessing the leader didn't ask you any questions about you and how you were doing.

Not authentic.

What does authenticity look like?

Working a room? Come on. I like to say that everyone is really interesting for at least three to five minutes. So engage authentically, learn something, and maybe teach something.

Authenticity looks like admitting failure. Everyone makes mistakes but a person who lives in the world authentically shares his or her mistakes, or values the role mistakes can make in becoming a more effective and productive organization.

• *Learn to Tell a Good Story:* I drive staff and board clients mad talking about this. A great leader is a great storyteller. I talk in the next chapter about this at great length, but it is absolutely critical and a key component of the coaching work I do with clients around commencement addresses and gala remarks. What kind of story? The kind of story that makes folks say, "Tell me more," or "Let me get out my checkbook," or "Now *that* is a story I should write about!" or "Will you come talk to my congressman?"

A great leader is a great storyteller. *Have Fun; Be Funny:* One of the reasons I started my blog (www.joangarry.com/) was that nearly every nonprofit resource was so damned serious. I get it. Saving the world is serious business. But that kind of intensity is not sustainable. You have to have a release valve. I find that behaving like an eight-year-old is often a very good strategy.

So we were in the midst of a board meeting and a quite serious discussion about the need for a greater investment in technology. Our IT director, Aasun Eble, who was indeed quite able, was in the midst of a serious and dry presentation. Seemingly out of nowhere, the slide shown in Figure 1.3 appeared.

FIGURE 1.3 You can never go wrong with pets in a board presentation.

Aasun decided we should all meet his three poodles. The room became weak with laughter. But that is not the end of the story.

From that day forward, you did not give a board presentation at a GLAAD board meeting without a picture of your pets appearing somewhere on a slide. This gimmick brought my senior staff to life for our board in a way that resonated for them. It was no longer the CFO or the director of IT. It was Kerry, the dad to two adorable kittens, Marilyn and Monroe. And it was unexpected and funny. It brought us together in a different sort of way.

- *Be Bold:* I believe that with authenticity and conviction comes a sense of fearlessness. Now I'm not suggesting that you suggest a bold, new strategy or initiative in your first week (that would be stupid, not bold). I'm suggesting that your board, your staff, and your constituents or clients deserve a leader who will make the tough calls, or come up with a new idea and try it. I'm not talking about arrogance here, nor am I talking about a leader who behaves like a lone cowboy. But remember: Didn't you step into a leadership role to *change* the status quo?

- *Be Joyful:* Related, but different from humor. This should not be that hard to feel or to project.

I have a beef with executive directors who don't see their work as a privilege. To get paid to do something that matters? To make a living making some part of the world a better place? I'm not naive; the work can be hard, painful, and sometimes feel like too steep a climb. But make no mistake. It's a joy and a privilege and the most effective nonprofit leaders see it that way and it's palpable.

Did you just read the list and remember wistfully that Dino's Pizzeria is looking for drivers.

Don't give up on me so easily.

Remember: Nobody has all these from the start.

These attributes can be developed and you can present them in your own way.

These attributes do not *replace* skills. I am just arguing that attributes are often ignored as you consider your own leadership bag of tricks. But working on cultivating these attributes can have as much, if not more, of a payoff than a class on how to read a balance sheet or to help you show off a certificate in nonprofit fundraising.

THE *REAL* POWER OF LEADERSHIP

I saved the most important lesson for last. Understanding how power works as a nonprofit leader is critical. Realizing that developing your core attributes in addition to skills can take your leadership game from good to great.

But never forget where the real power comes from.

It comes from the two to three sentences that you and your board slaved over and nearly wordsmithed to a pulp: your mission. What is it you do and *what is it in the service of.*

> But never forget where the real power comes from . . . your mission statement is your North Star.

Your mission statement is your North Star. The big thing that matters most. Your role as a leader is to keep the organization focused on it, even when you are deciding about the centerpieces for the gala.

We'll talk more about mission statements in the next chapter but here's one quick example:

> *Make-A-Wish Foundation:* We grant the wishes of children with life-threatening medical conditions to enrich the human experience with hope, strength, and joy.

As a leader of this organization, you are not only in the wish-granting business for a really sick kid (of course, that alone would be enough). But there is more to it.

Every wish *enriches the human experience*, not just of the struggling individual. Every wish lifts us all up. When we read one of that organization's stories, we feel a certain pride in what it means to be human. It brings us joy. And hope. Just like the mission statement says.

Great nonprofit leaders have certain skills, work on honing core attributes, and develop not only a real understanding of the nature of nonprofit power but an appreciation for it as well.

I don't mean to make it sound so simple or easy—it's not. Like I said, you are in the mountain-moving business—it couldn't possibly be easy. But with your mission as your beacon, it is worth every single minute.

"Your nonprofit dynamically disseminates an expanded array of potentialities to continually initiate distinctive infrastructures? I don't get it."

Chapter 2 You've Got to Get Me at Hello

Some organizations are easier to explain to folks than others. An organization that helps clients directly would seem to be the easiest. Advocacy and lobbying often feel more complex and abstract. Schools can struggle to identify messages that clearly differentiate them from other choices parents have for their kids.

But get this: Even the easy ones don't always get it right.

One of my clients is an easy organization to talk about. Very easy, actually. The organization delivers nutritious, high-quality meals to folks with serious illnesses. They also provide counseling and nutrition education to clients and their families.

Cities and towns all across America have organizations like this—lots of volunteers taking care of friends and neighbors who can't quite take care of themselves. It's what I love about nonprofit work. At its best, people come together to take care of one another.

So this client asked me to come in and help build the fundraising capacity of its board. Consultants often start by talking about the total universe of philanthropic dollars, how generous people are, and, of course, the slide every consultant has in her deck:

Q: "What is the Number One reason people do not give to causes they care about?"
A: Because they are not asked.

When I work with my clients, I take a different approach.

I begin with a cocktail party—except there are no cocktails and the only guest is me. It's a cocktail party for your organization and the premise is that I know precious little. Like oh so many people who attend such events, I come because of the view of Central Park from the terrace of the fabulous apartment, or the open bar, or both.

I say to each person, one by one: So tell me about your organization.

The only direction they are given? Be succinct. Make me care. Make it stick.

Here's how it played out with the staff of a Meals-on-Wheels organization.

"We deliver hundreds of meals each week, each of them tailored to the needs of our clients."

Good. Data is good because size *does* matter. But data alone does not stick with me.

"We pride ourselves in never turning anyone away."

Okay, impressive. But if you don't have to turn anyone away, tell me again why you need my money?

> "Our food is delicious. And we can customize meals for specific kinds of illnesses."

Okay, we're getting warmer. We're not just getting food out the door. We care about our clients enough to be sure the food is delicious. I like this a lot.

No one was wrong. Every staff member spoke passionately about the work. I was inspired and it was clear that this organization was lucky to have each and every one of them.

But I'll be honest; I am not an easy grader. I wanted more. I wanted to touch and feel the work. And I was looking for more context.

There were five missing elements of the recipe.

1. Emotion

    What emotion do clients experience? Or the folks in the kitchen or on the trucks? In two or three minutes, can you take me on a tour?

    > "Our organization feeds people. It creates a community of caring people who feed and are fed by each other. We bring thousands of families hope each week. We deliver companionship and our delicious food is a gift."

2. Real People

    > "For 20 years, Bob has been driving one of our trucks. He has the same route and talks about his families like, well, like family. He returns to the office and stops in the kitchen to tell the crew that

Mary (give her a disease and an age) loved the cranberry sauce. She said it tasted like the kind her mom made."

3. *Add Dose of Need and Urgency* (here's where you can add in size and data):

"When we started our work, we delivered X meals a year. This coming year, we are budgeted to increase that to Y meals. Government funding has decreased in the last Z years, increasing our urgent need for private dollars."

4. *Then Add You* (seal the deal with personal experience):

"Today, I'm a staff member, but I started as a kitchen volunteer. The soup I helped prepare was so much more than soup. It's hope, compassion. I know we are really feeding people. I saw it firsthand when I rode the truck to make deliveries once a month. We had this one client—Madeline—a feisty woman in her early seventies fighting cancer. She was one tough bird. But when we arrived, she melted. Her whole face lit up. And she told us the soup was almost as good as her own."

5. Stir and Voilà!

You have me at hello. I am drawn in. I want to know more. I may be ready to actually *do!*

> Even for an organization whose mission is crystal clear and the impact is quantifiable, it can be tough to tell a good story.

* * *

Even for an organization whose mission is crystal clear and the impact is quantifiable, it can be tough to tell a good story.

But I know this in my heart. Anytime someone utters the magic words, *"Tell me about your organization,"* you are being handed a big, fat opportunity.

And if I have anything to say about it, you won't miss it.

TELL ME ABOUT YOUR ORGANIZATION

I just said that this question is a big, fat opportunity. Allow me to explain. Whether you are staff, board, faculty, administration, or a volunteer, you are a singularly credible messenger and one of the most powerful ambassadors your organization has.

Through your telling, you can bring volunteers, other board members, elected officials, parents, clients, donors, and press to the organization you care so much about.

So you have to get this right.

Talking about your organization in a way that is compelling, engaging, and memorable is, in my mind, the most important skill you can develop.

You are thinking to yourself, *I don't often have time to tell a whole story*. Or more importantly, I was asked the question but only have a minute. We're standing in a lobby.

Different settings demand different tellings.

IN THE LOBBY—THE MISSION STATEMENT

Let me be crystal clear. A mission statement is not a story. It's also not an elevator pitch. It is a written declaration of purpose. It should state clearly who you serve, what you do, and why you do it.

It rarely changes. (If a need exists for a new mission statement, it the a result of some kind of significant strategic shift—more on that in Chapter 4.)

Charity: Water, for example, will likely always exist *"To bring clean, safe drinking water to people in developing countries."*

Right to the point, eh? The statement articulates the problem and offers hope with Charity: Water on the job.

Teach for America: *"Growing the movement of leaders who work to ensure that kids growing up in poverty get an excellent education."*

What I like about this is that it makes its two-fold purpose clear—to grow a movement of education leaders and to ensure that kids in poverty get first-rate education. This is a good one.

NPR: *"To work in partnership with member stations to create a more informed public—one challenged and invigorated by a deeper understanding and appreciation of events, ideas, and cultures."*

What I like about this one is that it is aspirational. I desperately want the public to be well informed and I only have to hit *scan* on the radio or graze through TV news to know that NPR represents hope. I know what this organization stands for. I know it will take me deeper into the news, that it will help me better understand and appreciate the world around me.

Sadly, mission statements don't often rise to the occasion.

That last sentence was oh so kind. Many mission statements are big hot messes.

They are developed by a group of Type A folks (board and senior staff) who become frighteningly tied to individual words and phrases. Words like *facilitate* (weak), *integrate* (unclear), *change-agent* (does that mean you represent people who make change?)

It can get ugly. And the outcome uglier still.

As a result, precious few of the 1.5 million nonprofits in America have a five-star mission statement. Typically, your best hope is for clinical and soulless and, at worst, you get completely incomprehensible.

So in that context, how does a mission statement fare in the telling?

Well, first things first. Mission statements often come across a lot like the Girl or Boy Scout pledge said with three fingers in the air and hand over heart. Memorized, regurgitated, and often without meaning.

And by the way, open any conversation with a possible stakeholder with the words "Our mission is . . ." and watch said stakeholder's eyes roll into the back of her head. Watch opportunity fly away.

A clear mission statement is absolutely critical to every single stakeholder group, and is one of the key ingredients to a healthy nonprofit.

But a story it is not.

And that's okay. You are just in the lobby.

Mission statements are okay in lobbies. But if you are one of the unlucky nonprofits with a long, incomprehensive mission statement, offer the one you'd write if you were solely in charge.

IN THE ELEVATOR—THE PITCH

Okay, now you are in the elevator and the same question is posed. You have a greater opportunity, but it's not the kind that comes with sitting next to someone at a dinner party. It's somewhere in between.

In this situation, a mission statement will not do, especially if you have one of those really bad ones.

Note that you are not in the full-on solicitation business here. You don't have enough time. So what is the goal? To inform and to *invite*.

> **Get the facts out quickly—short and to the point— and then say something compelling that makes them want to know more—that invites them into a conversation.**

You have 30 seconds, maybe 60 if you are lucky.

A few pointers:

- *No mission statement.* Do not attempt to impress this person with a recitation of your mission statement. This is not impressive. We call this a bad move, a missed opportunity.
- *Pretend your audience is a 10-year-old kid.* One time, I asked an executive director to tell me about her organization. We were at a cocktail party (not in an elevator). *Twenty minutes later,* she finally wrapped it up.

  I couldn't help myself. I asked her a question. Do you think you might answer that question again and, this time, pretend I am 10?

  It was shorter. She cut out all the jargon. She spoke simply and clearly. And there was something about my being 10 that led her to speak to *me,* to think about *me* and what would engage me. It became *way* less about her organization and her and much more about me.
- *End with a real invitation.* It could be in the form of a question: *"Would you like to know more?"* It could be the exchange of business cards. Or *"Can I get your email address and follow up?"*

  Are you thinking—*one minute and I'm going to get an email address*? Well, you sure ain't if you don't ask.

For a variety of examples of nonprofit elevator pitches—good, bad and otherwise—head to joangarry.com/elevator-pitches and you'll find dozens in the comments section along with my feedback on each.

STEP OFF THE ELEVATOR AND WORK THE ROOM

As with my fundraising trainings, this is the big, fat opportunity. Unconstrained by that short elevator ride or the quick chat in the lobby, you are now free to chat for a few minutes with individuals.

Let's assume it is not a fundraiser for your organization—you're at a cocktail party or a barbeque. You know some folks and not others.

First things first, put on your organizational glasses. Look at the attendees through the lens of your role with your nonprofit.

Now I don't mean this in some kind of icky way. I'm not suggesting you make a beeline for your neighbor who just got a big new job. I'm talking about *connections*, not *capacity* (something we will talk about in Chapter 5 on fundraising and your board).

Before you begin to chat someone up, remember something important. Most people are not engaged as a board member or a donor or a volunteer. These people very much admire people who are. They will find your involvement inspiring.

If you tell a good story.

And if you tell a great story, it may move them from inspired to motivated. That is the home run.

DOIN' WHAT DOES NOT COME NATURALLY

There are two universal challenges faced by board, staff, and volunteer ambassadors of every single nonprofit.

Fortunately, they are both very simple and very easy to remedy.

1. The Curse of Knowledge

In 1990, a Stanford graduate conducted a series of experiments that revealed something quite profound and obvious all at the same time. Through certain experiments, she was able to unearth that once we know something, we find it hard to imagine not knowing it. Our knowledge has "cursed" us. We have difficulty sharing it with others because we can't readily re-create their state of mind.

This curse came to light in the work of Chip and Dan Heath in a 1990 *Harvard Business Review* article and in a subsequent book I highly recommend called *Made to Stick*.

And you will never guess what the antidote is to this curse. The Heath brothers are clear:

> "Leaders can thwart the curse of knowledge by 'translating' their strategies into concrete language." They continue: "Stories, too, work particularly well in dodging the curse of knowledge, because they force us to use concrete language."

I rest my first case.

2. The Elements of a Good Story

I come from solid Irish stock. We are hardwired to tell a good story. (We are also hardwired to enjoy it more than the folks we tell it to, but I digress.)

But you have to know what makes a good story to tell one. And not all nonprofit leaders have the gift of Irish gab and the temperament to attempt to enthrall a crowd.

So allow me to share what I have learned about good storytelling from my experience, my ancestors, and my remarkable clients.

Let's start with the don'ts.

Don't Assume

Chip and Dan Heath make this point quite clearly in their book but I'll offer a personal example. I was working with an organization that fights hunger in my home state of New Jersey. Now, I live in an affluent suburb of New Jersey and experience all the privilege that comes with it. I'm lucky. My view is also somewhat myopic. If this organization is going to tell a story to motivate me, a personal story will get me, but don't assume I know the magnitude of this problem in my own backyard.

> According to the most recent census, of the 8.8 million residents of New Jersey, nearly 1.2 million of them experience food insecurity. Then consider that nearly half a million of those people are kids.

If you assume I know that, you miss a huge opportunity to motivate me.

Don't Give Me a List

Lists don't stick. Big things do. Let's look for a minute at AIDS services organizations. At the highest level, we know that these organizations work to fight AIDS. Their vision is a world without it.

Most HIV/AIDS organizations today have a very long list of services they provide to folks living with HIV—on the direct service side, you will find legal clinics, mental health services, substance abuse programs, programs specifically for different demographics, HIV testing, syringe access programs, and workforce development.

Amazing list of services, right? Impressive. But I'm not going to hold on to all of them. And I don't really have a through line—a common thread.

Don't hit me with a list. Try something like this:

> "At XYZ organization, we understand that a life with HIV is a journey. We are there at every step of the way. We also know that it affects every aspect of your life. If your journey involves substance abuse, we are there. Housing discrimination? We are there. Need a hot meal? Join our community for lunch or dinner seven nights a week. At XYZ, we take care of all of you."

Don't Lead with Your Vision

I hope your organization has one. Sadly, many don't. But let's just say you do.

If you start with vision, you can either emotionally paralyze the listener or cause them to shut down.

Try this: *We are working to end human slavery worldwide.*

Of course, I am impressed. In fact, I'm so impressed, I'm probably speechless. What question do I ask as a follow-up? I don't know how to jump in to make this a conversation. Remember you are inviting folks to join you in a conversation about the organization. Try to avoid shutting them down.

> Remember you are inviting folks to join you in a conversation about the organization.

I'm going to take my own advice here and not assume.

Let's talk about the elements of a powerful and compelling story. And to make my point, I will tell the story of my friends Ken and Judy and an organization in New York City called Transportation Alternatives.

> "If the story is not about the hearer, he will not listen. A great and interesting story is about everyone or it will not last."
> —*John Steinbeck,*
> East of Eden

Someone to Root For

Judy tells the story of Transportation Alternatives, the community they have built, and the impact they have had. My friend Judy lost her daughter Ella, who was hit by a New York City bus. I've known this family since Ella and our daughter Scout met weekly in a local playgroup. Ella was special.

Judy is our protagonist. Her story is tragic. And my credibility as a messenger is very high because of my personal connection. And you want to know more.

Struggle or Conflict

"The only thing that kept Judy and Ken 'alive' was a need to do something—anything—to make that Brooklyn intersection safer. It had already been identified as one of the most dangerous in the city. But how could they get anyone to pay attention? So much bureaucracy. So much red tape. And they felt they were fighting the battle alone."

The struggle is clear. They want changes to the intersection. No one is paying attention to them.

Empathy

> "I admire Ken and Judy so much. This could have been my daughter. Or yours. I'd like to think that I would focus on securing a legacy for my daughter."

This is an important part. Put the listener in the shoes of that protagonist. God forbid, if *you* were Judy and Ken, what would you want?

How Is Your Organization Working to Solve This Problem?

> "Transportation Alternatives created an army of the bereaved—a community in which the words 'I know what you are going through' really meant something. The organization worked with this group to create a goal. A different one from Ken and Judy's—one it believed, based on their understanding of New York City politics—was actually achievable. They secured buy-in from the army and in less than three months, the new goal was met. The speed limit in New York City was dropped from 30 mph to 25 mph."

What have we learned? Transportation Alternatives was compassionate and empathetic and worked with this group to help them, to offer them hope, to help them attempt to find some good in unimaginable loss. The organization worked with the group to set a tangible goal and met it in record time. It makes you want to write a check right now, doesn't it?

Evidence of Forward Motion with New Goals

> "Empowered by this remarkable accomplishment, the TA army set new goals. Their next stop is the bus drivers union and the Taxi and Limousine Commission, to tackle the issue of enforcement. And yes, there is talk of replicating this model in other cities."

I totally get this organization. I recognize TA as caring and compassionate and also driven to make a change that honors the legacy of children taken too soon. But not only driven. Smart, diplomatic, and intentional. An organization with measurable impact (speed limit) and immeasurable impact (offering hope to families broken by loss).

This is how it works.

TWO MORE EXAMPLES FOR EMPHASIS

Two more examples that I hope will help you in crafting your own. One from the for-profit sector and one from my very own backyard. Both of these stories are true.

FedEx

We all know the unique selling proposition of FedEx. "Absolutely positively overnight." Late one afternoon, a driver (let's call her Judy) had truck trouble. Her truck broke down. FedEx has a plan for such things (of course) and sent a replacement van. But it was stuck in traffic.

Judy loves working for FedEx and lives its mission every day. She begins to deliver a few packages on foot but can see that she will simply run out of time.

Now I'm not sure what I would do in this circumstance— would I call my boss and say I had tried everything but that on this day, I could not meet the delivery promise? I bet some people would do that.

Not Judy. She managed to persuade a *competitor's* driver to take her to her last stops.

In My Own Backyard

When our kids were younger, they attended a small, progressive school in suburban New Jersey.

Our twins, Ben and Kit, are thick as thieves and always have been.

When they were five, the school thought maybe they were *too* thick. The teachers, who knew them each so well, determined that two separate pre-K experiences made sense.

Try telling that to Kit. She was bereft. Miserable. The sweetest kid in the world actually bit a teacher. It got pretty bad.

In other schools, a kid who bites might be removed from the class. Certainly a punishment of some sort was in order.

But Kit's teachers proposed a better solution—one that was so smart, so simple, and so compassionate, I will never forget it.

Twice a week, Kit would get on the phone and call Ben's classroom and invite Ben up for snack time. He'd come into the classroom and Kit would already have set out his Goldfish crackers and juice for him. They both lit up. All was well with the world. They would chat for a while and then Ben would toddle back to his class.

I still get goose bumps when I think about how wonderful these teachers were to propose a solution like this. How much they cared.

* * *

A story like this is golden. It speaks to the mission of the school, to what makes it a unique and special place. Even if you don't have kids, you want them to go to a place that makes these kinds of choices. And Kit, as the protagonist, is clear about her challenge and the school solves her problem in a way that honors her.

PRACTICE, KID, PRACTICE

Because storytelling does not come naturally to organizational ambassadors, as I mentioned earlier, a nonprofit organization must work with intention to build a culture of storytelling in its organization.

Each board and staff member should understand the elements of a good story and be asked to shape her or his own. Here are some ideas:

- Set aside time at a board meeting to ask people to share their organization stories. Offer each other constructive feedback. Which story stayed with you? Does it bring the work to life? Is the impact clear?
- Consider quarterly brown bag lunches with staff to practice as well. A simple question: *What do you do, why is it important, and what is one illustration of tangible impact?* Give each staffer two to three minutes, tops.
- Not only do staff members fine-tune storytelling skills but they also hear a variety of stories they themselves could tell.

- Regularly feed your board and staff with new (current) stories about the organization that they can use when at a weekend barbeque or a fundraiser for another organization. Your best ambassadors need good, fresh material!

Have you ever sat at a tactical, in-the-weeds staff meeting for 90 minutes, headed back to your desk, and realized no one told a single great story about the impact of the work of the organization?

When I suggest this to nonprofit E.D.s, they often seem as if it never crossed their minds. *"Oh, that's a good idea!"* they will tell me.

So just do it. Build a culture of storytelling in your organization and it can make all the difference in the world.

In Chapter 3, I'll focus on the role of the board chair and her relationship to the E.D., but I'll give you an appetizer here.

It is the shared job of the board chair and the executive director to ensure that the key ambassadors of the organizations are also your best storytellers.

> It is the shared job of the board chair and the executive director to ensure that the key ambassadors of the organizations are also your best storytellers.

Here's a simple equation. If you keep it on a Post-it note on your desk and incorporate it into working with your board, your volunteers, and your staff at all levels, I guarantee you will bring more motivated folks to your organization's table.

Credible Messenger + Compelling Story = A New Stakeholder

"You actually made a piñata of your board chair as a team building exercise at your retreat? That's hilarious. But I think you're going to need extra sessions."

Chapter 3 Co-Pilots in a Twin-Engine Plane

So, tell me the one thing that illustrates that your organization is thriving. Just one. No fair, you say? Hey! It's my book. Just one. Here's your list.

- A strong mission
- A solid cash reserve
- A charismatic executive director
- The diversity of your revenue streams
- A low staff turnover percentage

What? You can't pick just one? I'm going to make it even harder. The answer is not on this list. But I'll give you a hint. It's a *relationship*.

In my experience with hundreds of nonprofits, it's clear to me that the single most important indicator of a healthy nonprofit is the relationship between the staff and the board leader—the executive director (E.D.) and the board chair.

Why?

It's simple.

> **Shared leadership with an invested thought partner with leadership skills can cut many challenges off at the pass.**

So E.D.s reading this are thinking—"Hey wait! I'm in charge and things work best when I am just left to my own devices to run the organization and the board just raises money." And board chairs are in a different place—"On paper, I am the boss. I'm not buying this 'shared leadership' thing—at the end of the day, I am responsible for hiring and firing our E.D.—that doesn't feel like a partnership to me."

I thought perhaps I had dispelled these ideas in Chapter 1 when I spoke about where power comes from in a nonprofit, but we need to keep digging on this one because it is (a) important and (b) a bit counterintuitive.

The E.D. and the board chair each lead a group of the organization's most vital stakeholders. The E.D. manages a staff (if the organization is lucky enough to have such resources) paid to do the critical day-to-day work of the organization. Unlike a corporate board, a nonprofit board adds remarkable horsepower to the organization (no eye rolling please—stay with me!). With the proper recruitment strategy, a board becomes a volunteer army of the highest caliber, with stakeholders who bring skills, expertise, and life experience that the organization desperately needs and would not likely be able to afford. And, ideally, each and every one of them shares a passion for the mission and determination to do what it takes to ensure that the organization has the highest degree of impact. Lastly, each understands her or his role as an ambassador for the organization, always on the lookout for new stakeholders—the best and the brightest staff, donors, sponsors, other volunteers—to continue to build the capacity of the organization to do its very best work.

It sounds like a great model, doesn't it? Board and staff working as thought partners who, together, drive the organization forward led by two individuals who understand their roles, both separately and in relation to one another, each of whom are passionate about their jobs and determined to do right by the organization.

It could be.

It should be.

And you're not buying it. And to be blunt, you (and I'm talking to you board and staff leaders) are not always committed to investing the time and energy into getting it right.

I argue it is your job. Your clients and the communities you advocate for deserve your best. And while it is messy, this shared leadership model is the key to enabling nonprofits of all sizes to have greater reach and impact.

But here's the thing: In what I consider to be the ultimate irony, these two groups are far too often in tension with each other. Tension. Not just peaceful co-existence. Tension. In fact, it is this tension that led me to become a certified mediator. In working with clients with organizational challenges, it isn't long before I find my way to the organizational leadership. And there, I often find a relationship that is not working. The roles are not clear, the communication is poor and the expectations are either unrealistic or unstated.

There, I said it. It's like a marriage on the rocks.

I'm by no means suggesting that creating and sustaining this kind of partnership is easy. One of my blog subscribers put it well: "The board chair and the E.D. need to be in step like in a three-legged race." The last time I was in a three-legged race, I was probably 10 and it wasn't pretty. But the winners managed through the challenge, sometimes caused their partners to fall, helped each other up, and crossed the finish line, joyful about winning and probably laughing about how filthy they were.

> "The board chair and the E.D. need to be in step like in a three-legged race."

THE IDEAL BOARD CHAIR PROFILE

Based on what we have talked about so far, it seems to me that you are looking for someone green (à la Kermit), whose love of the cause is actually greater than her fear of asking for "green" and who actually *wanted* the job. We need someone who has enough of an ego to want to be successful, and yet is humble enough to understand that everyone's voice matters and who, as I mentioned in Chapter 2, values the power that comes from those around her. Lastly, you want someone who manages the executive director by asking good questions and encouraging the discussion of missteps, and who gives the E.D. the right amount of rope.

At my very first board meeting as an E.D., I was delighted to be supported by two co-chairs who, in my mind, fit this bill to a tee: so smart, so strategic, so committed, fundraising champions. The two of them were part of the package that sold me on leaving the for-profit sector to take this great, new low-paying job. We had a terrific first meeting that we had designed together. We had a clear sense of what the outcomes needed to be.

Except one.

At the end of the meeting, they both resigned. Thank goodness thought balloons are not visible to the naked eye. I was furious. They had betrayed me.

Nope. They did me a favor. They told the group that they had micromanaged my predecessor as a result of concerns of performance issues and did not believe they could give me sufficient rope. I needed and deserved the right amount of rope to lead and build the organization.

So what did I do? I had to think on my feet. What did I need to do to: (1) raise cash and (2) build the board? With these as my priorities, I identified two board members who were aggressive fundraisers, invested in my success, and knew a million people. If we could do these two things *together,* we could stabilize the organization and begin to attract board prospects who would see board leadership as a privilege. The strategy paid off. Within a year, I had a five-star board chair and we built a partnership and an organization to last.

RECRUITING THE IDEAL BOARD CHAIR

This section is going to be really short. Ninety-five percent of my clients don't recruit board members for leadership abilities. Certainly not the attributes that work in the nonprofit space (for shorthand, shall we just call them the "green" ones?). I'll talk more about the shared responsibility of board building, but here I just want to call out the insecurity and timidity with which most boards recruit colleagues. Recruitment is a process in which obligations are soft-peddled. One client told me that a potential rock star board member was recruited with this language: *Don't worry, this is a really easy board to be on.* Do you think this board member became a rock star? Simple answer: no. Recruitment is all about who I can get rather than who I need.

Board service is then implicitly (or in the case of my client mentioned earlier) soft-peddled as not very important. And I don't know about you, but my "not very important stuff" is at the bottom of my list.

And then when it is time to field a candidate for board chair, your organization is in trouble. If you recruit this way, a great leader joins your board by accident, not intention. It's time to put on your "grownup pants" and recruit with intention—to go and find those folks with leadership skills and sell them on the difference they can make.

> Dear Joan,
> My current board chair is stepping down and I am bereft. He was terrific. He gave generously and he left me alone to do my thing. I didn't talk to him much, and he protected me from meddlesome board members with crazy ideas. My new board chair has already said she wants weekly meetings—I am sensing a five-star micromanager.
>
> Signed,
> Just Leave Me Alone

"Leave Me Alone" turned out to be totally wrong. She traded a well-meaning, dedicated board chair that was a bit of an absentee landlord for a real partner. And there is no question that the growth and the success of the organization can be tied back. So what did the partner have that made it work?

THE FIVE-STAR BOARD CHAIR CHECKLIST

Here's who you need to go find. Maybe the person is already on your board (wouldn't that be nice?). If not, it is the Number Two priority of the organization (right after finding a five-star staff leader). Here's what it takes to be a five-star board chair.

- *Interest.* Seems like a pretty obvious quality, but a reluctant board chair doesn't work.
- *Passion for the Mission.* The board leader has to be crazy about the work of the organization.
- *Time.* Now, most Type A board members being considered for leadership positions are so busy they can barely breathe. That doesn't mean they don't have time. My best board chair was ridiculously busy in her day job but we planned and she understood the commitment she was making to work closely with me. She made the time. And not just on the phone. We met face to face to talk and would allow more time for the less tactical and the more strategic.
- *Schedule Autonomy.* Meetings are typically scheduled. But things come up that require board chair attention. If you have a boss who drags you into meetings with regularity and does so with precious little notice, this can be a problem for an E.D. with a pressing issue. And frustrating too. Because E.D. schedules are no less challenging.
- *Diplomacy.* Can you hear a really stupid comment or question without rolling your eyes? Board members are a mixed bag. They are volunteers and don't always have the knowledge to combine with the enthusiasm. Their enthusiasm must be honored. But at the same time, a great board chair must diminish expectations that anything will likely come of the idea.
- *Asking Tough Questions Well.* I'm going to put it out there. E.D.s have thinner skin than you think. They get defensive. After all, they know their organization backward and forward. You? You're just a volunteer. You don't know what it's really like. It can be very unflattering. Board chairs need to, in that context, learn how to ask smart, constructive questions that

lead to productive conversations rather than a 15-minute defense. This could be a separate bullet, but it is this kind of attribute that leads to the trust necessary to partner in such a way that you talk through not just what works, but what isn't working.

- *Serve as a Fundraising Champion.* Board members will follow your lead. If you are out creating connections through your sphere of influence, board members will see what that looks like. And if they choose not to go that route, it won't be because they don't see what that looks like.

- *Motivate Volunteers to Deliver.* Done properly, today's committee chairs are tomorrow's board leaders. Have the chairs worked with their committees to set annual goals, to identify a project they want to work on. Do they meet regularly? How is attendance? What kind of agenda is circulated? How is the meeting facilitated? Far too often, the staff liaison takes responsibility for the meeting agenda and the forward motion at the meeting. That's not her or his role.

- *Recognize the Value of Appreciation.* When something happens, are you going to be able to make time to shoot an email to staff ASAP? More importantly, can you command the attention of the board to encourage them to do the same? I can't tell you how demoralizing it is for staff to send out exciting news and get total and complete radio silence from the board. At first, E.D.s confirm that the email has gone out. Then they just assume you don't care.

> I can't tell you how demoralizing it is for staff to send out exciting news and get total and complete radio silence from the board.

- *Understand the Value of Accountability.* The role of board chair is a delicate one indeed. With committee chairs and especially your E.D., it's true that the buck really stops with you. But in a world of shared leadership, you lead to develop goals and success metrics together and similarly evaluate them together—Shared leadership and shared accountability.

THE TELLTALE SIGNS OF WRONG

I get it. Kermit is not in the boardroom. Your board chair is highly flawed. Or is she? How do you know? I'm amazed at how often folks write me to ask if this how a board chair should behave and the behavior described is outrageous. And so, in the spirit of bringing the "wrong" to light, here are some behaviors that readers have written to me about. Each of them represents a big, fat flag on the field. In aggregate, it's hot mess.

- Your board chair was volun*told* to take the role and constantly complains about how much time the role takes.
- When someone suggests the board use Robert's Rules of Order, the board chair says casually, *"Who's Robert?"*
- Your board president announces, "The only people I have ever led are my family."
- As the E.D., you have not had a performance evaluation in more than two years.
- The board chair believes the E.D. should create the agenda for the board meetings.
- The board chair solicits ideas for the board meeting from the board members rather than designing the agenda strategically. (You can only imagine the ideas that get generated with no guidance.)
- The board chair checks in for about five minutes every few days and says, *"So what's going on?"*
- The board chair is the executive director's best friend.
- You overhear the board chair at an event. He is being asked about the size of the annual budget and the number of full-time

employees. He is clueless. He finally sputters out: *"I need to introduce you to our executive director."*

- The board chair sends the E.D. flowers on National Secretary's Day and is not being ironic.
- Your board chair, in a discussion about trimming costs, asks the E.D. how old her assistant is.

PLAYING THE HAND YOU ARE DEALT

I was close to my grandmother. Kitty lived a bike ride away and I could while away the afternoon with Irish breakfast tea and a few hands of Canasta—a very warm memory, but a distant one. Kitty Conlon taught me (among many other things) that you can win handily (pun intended) with a less-than-ideal hand.

So let's say that your staff leader is good but not great, or is good with great tendencies, or great with vulnerabilities. Let's say your board chair was *"voluntold"* or as I like to say, made the unfortunate choice of heading to the restroom while the vote took place. How do I play *this* hand to win? Because the truth of the matter is, the preceding scenario is the most likely one you will encounter during your tenure in either role. Ideal is good to stretch for but as Elliott said in the movie *E.T.*, as he flew on a bicycle with an extraterrestrial being in the basket, *"This is reality!"*

Here's what you have going for you: Both of you want to do a good job and care deeply about the organization. This can get you a long way.

Dear Joan,

I have been on the board for a little over a year and was recently elected board president. I don't believe I'm exactly qualified for this role, but our board is struggling with leadership and, to be honest, no one has any guts. So I was the only person nominated and felt obligated to accept. I'm somewhat happy to take on this role but I work, have two small kids, and I'm just one person. I really care about the organization and want to do a good job. Where do I start?

Signed,
Gutsy or Stupid

So here's the deal, Gutsy. Get on line behind thousands of folks who have stood or are standing in your shoes. Take it one step at a time and let your love of your organization lead the way.

GET IT RIGHT FROM THE START

- Prepare to Allocate a *Lot* of Time in the First 30 Days
  I mean it. What you do in the first 30 days of *any* new job sets the tone for the work moving forward. No different here.
- Set Up a Three-Hour Meeting—Just the Two of You (or three if there are co-chairs or a vice chair). This may be the best investment of time you make during your leadership partnership. Here are the basics you should cover:
  - *Review Job Descriptions*—It's easy to find sample descriptions on the Internet and use them as the basis for a conversation about where the roles are separate and where they overlap.
  - *Review List of Board Members*—Talk about their strengths and weaknesses. Talk about how you might rearrange the deck chairs and who is worth investing in for future leadership.
  - *Review List of Senior Staff*—This is where thought partnership comes in. The E.D. is responsible for the staff but let the

board chair in as a mentor and coach. Let her partner with you in thinking about moving your staff from good to great.

- *Review Board Fundraising*—Have the E.D. bring a document that outlines board fundraising—in its aggregate and by person. Talk about needs, opportunities, the role of the development committee in holding its peers accountable, and discuss if tools or trainings are needed.
- *Agree on a Weekly Meeting*—Yes, I said weekly. At least at first. I recommend that the E.D. prepare a simple agenda and send it the night before the meeting. Get your calendars out and schedule the first six. Lock 'em in and commit to each other that they will happen. Not sure what to put on the agenda? It should be modeled exactly on the 7-point agenda here: www.joangarry.com/ceo-board-chair-relationship/.

• Set Up Time with the Former Chair

Yes, more time. Sorry. But another key investment. Learn about the experience. You'll learn about what to do. And what not to do.

• Reach Out to Every Board Member for 30 to 45 Minutes, Tops
- Why did you join the board?
- How has the experience been for you so far?
- How can I as the chair better support you?
- Critique our board meetings.
- Make requests—whatever they may be based on the three hours with the E.D.
- Finish this statement: "In order for us to be successful as a board in the next 12 months, I believe our board needs to _____."
- Thank them for their service (even if you hope they resign tomorrow).

• Set Two to Four Goals for Yourself

I've been working with a fine board chair. We had lunch just as he was taking on the role of chair. He told me that one of his key goals for the coming year was to take real steps to create a more effective board.

I saw him a few days ago. He has reconfigured the executive committee (with buy-in from all parties). He is reconfiguring board meetings to make them more enriching for the board members and less taxing on the staff. He has even managed to put someone who loves fundraising in the role of development committee chair (he's not just a board chair—he may also be a miracle worker). These are terrific examples of board chair goals. And, no, you can't have him.

- Buy a Copy of *Robert's Rules of Order* and Read It.

It really is embarrassing when the chair does not use them and follow them. It's a simple thing and maybe you operate less formally. But a board member at a meeting that is following them knows she is at a real meeting where real things happen.

(P.S. The guy's last name was Robert, not his first name).

THE PARTNERSHIP IN ACTION: THE DEVIL IS IN THE DETAILS

Build the Board

I'm not gonna lie. There is a lot of heavy lifting to do to build and "feed" a board. It will take both entities—board and staff leaders. It requires a commitment on all of your parts. Everyone needs to reach consensus of what a "high-functioning" board looks like and share an understanding that the effort of building one is mission critical. And no, Ms. E.D., a high-functioning board is *not* defined as one that raises a lot of money and then stays out of your hair.

> And no, Ms. E.D., a high-functioning board is *not* defined as one that raises a lot of money and then stays out of your hair.

A high-functioning board is an extension of the organization. At its best, it is a high-powered engine that drives the organization further than it could ever go with staff only. And because it is, in my humble opinion, an *extension and a partner* with the staff, the responsibility to ensure its highest possible function is shared.

This is not something I understood when I crossed the bridge to the nonprofit world. I saw the board as a collective supervisor and a fundraising engine. I think that was about as far as it went.

I needed to understand more, so I reached out to other E.D.s who had been around the block a long time (I highly recommend this in your first 30 days BTW). I sat with one particular E.D. who was generous with her time and her advice. She wanted me to succeed and she knew the climb would be steep. *"The best advice I can offer you is to go to every single board nominations/ recruitment meeting."*

While it felt counterintuitive to me (every minute I was not fundraising seemed like a waste of time to me), my colleague gave me a critical piece of advice and, being the good Catholic girl I was, I did what I was told.

Perhaps you are thinking her advice was Machiavellian in nature. Fill the board with allies who would agree with me and protect me. I'm sure that is how some would have interpreted the advice. I have seen that strategy put into play. The E.D. somehow grabs the power for board recruitment away from the board and, trust me, it can be catastrophic if the staff leader is a seriously poor performer and needs to go. Why catastrophic? It's time to cast a vote to fire the E.D. All in favor? A board built of individuals whose allegiance to the E.D. trumps allegiance to the organization will cast the wrong vote. I have seen it happen. Yet another reason that mediation certification comes in handy—too handy.

I heard something different in the sage advice from my colleague Lorri. The staff leader meets a broad swath of folks and will be, along with the development director, the best source of prospects. Lorri argued that I would get to know people, and learn what they may bring to the board table. In partnership with the board chair, we would know the skills and attributes we need. If I were not part of those meetings, my voice and an important perspective would be missing.

In that first year, I never missed a recruitment meeting. And the board members and I partnered to build an impressive board that was instrumental in building an organization to last.

What is complicated and dare I say "messy" is that the E.D. is responsible for who rides the staff "bus" and this is not in the purview of the board. Now this isn't to say that board members won't spend tons of time talking about the performance of this one or that one. Often legitimate, I might add. A special events manager is supposed to stay away from the bar and not dance topless with my six-year-old daughter (the memory of a lifetime for her, I might add). I get that. Concerns can be legitimate.

But an E.D. is evaluated based on the work, the staff she hires, and the impact the organization has. If she makes good hires, she is a star; bad hires, not so much.

But when it comes to getting the right people on the board bus, I argue that the work is a joint venture. Yes, the board will make the final decision, but the E.D. is a partner in this work with the board chair.

As I often say to E.D.s who complain about their boards (it is "sport" in the nonprofit community, btw): *The board you have is the board you build.*

Three Tips on "How"

1. Ensure the executive director is a standing member of the board recruitment and nominating committee. It is my hope that I drilled that into your heads in the preceding section.

2. Build and approve an ideal composition matrix. Can you imagine the general manager of the New York Yankees sending out scouts without a plan? Imagine this directive: *Go find some great ballplayers.* What would the recruiter do with that? Now consider this assignment: *We need a left-handed, middle-inning reliever. I need a power-hitting designated hitter who has a name that will sell tickets.* Well, *now* he has something to work with.

   The same goes for board members. Create a matrix of the ideal board and then talk about it at a full board meeting. Talk about skills, experience, and diversity, but don't forget attributes—diplomacy, facilitation skills, leadership potential. Without this, board members will hear this from the recruitment committee: "*I need two names from your Rolodex you think would make great board members.*" Two substantive problems here: (1) people don't have Rolodexes anymore and (2) board members need direction and clarity about what the board needs. And when you talk about it as a group, you all own the picture of the team that can make it to the World Series and everyone will be on the hunt for the folks who can fill the gap.

3. Engage the staff in the hunt. Executive directors, it's time to call you out. I apologize in advance but it will be worth it. You are all so busy blaming your board for, well, everything, that you forget something important: There are board prospects all around you. And who is equally likely to be interacting with them? Your staff!

   Need an event chair or vice chair? Or a corporate sponsor? Need someone with sector experience on your board? (You bet you do.) What about asking your lead program person? What about a longstanding volunteer or a program alum?

   When was the last time you as the E.D. had a staff meeting in which you enlisted help identifying great board members using the matrix approved by the board? I'm going to guess. Never? Hardly ever? You don't need to talk about it every week, but every month? You bet. It needs to be on the radar screen of every person—board and staff.

Okay, you have new board members in the house; now what?

Feed the Board

You have recruited strategically. You haven't begged anyone. You were clear about time and fundraising commitment and equally clear about the opportunity to work with amazing board and staff colleagues on an issue of deep significance to the new board member. You have a new cohort of board members that could shift the overall dynamics of your board.

I hate to break it to you, but your work in creating articulate ambassadors, strategic thought partners, fiscal stewards, and fundraising champions is just beginning. Now it is time to invest in them so that they can deliver.

Here are three core commitments that board and staff leaders must make together in order to maximize the new cohort.

1. Board Orientation

    You don't really think they remember anything they were told in the interview process, do you? Your job in a board orientation is several-fold:

    • *Inspire*—A board orientation without a "goose bump moment" is not a home run. Bring the work to life. A tour? A video you showed at the last gala? Something to open the meeting to remind their heart why they said yes.

    • *Educate*—They need to be ready to contribute from Day One. (No, Ms. Development Director, I am not talking about a check—*yet*.) The information they need includes an org chart, budget, strat plan, fundraising plan—you know what needs to be in there.

- *Stroke Egos*—Board members like to know they are in impressive company. They also like to feel like they have the inside scoop on the sector they care about. A board bio book includes not only CVs but also impressive profiles hits that mark. And maybe an article they have not seen about the future of the sector that gives them the ability to ignite their strategic thinking about where the organization lives in the larger sector and how it can be a central player.

2. Board Meeting

This a huge pet peeve of mine. I hear endless complaints about disengaged board members. I never take statements at face value but look for the underlying issue. I ask to see three or four past board meeting agendas. And then I sit with board chairs or E.D.s or both and ask them point blank, *"If you were a board member and attended each of these board meetings, would you be engaged?"* You grant their wish of keeping the board meetings short—*Why?* Board meetings that are painful should be short but a good board meeting should take the time necessary to feed the board with the nutrients they need to fulfill their responsibilities and most importantly, *to enable board members to feel like they are contributing in a three-dimensional way to the organization.*

Board members leave organizations because they feel like are being used or nagged (e.g., "I feel like a human ATM," "I get asked for everything but my opinion about marketing and that is what I *do* for a living").

Board and staff leaders, listen closely: board meetings are not necessary evils. They are major touch points your board members have with your organization. You need to make them count. Here's how (and, again, I'm not gonna lie—it requires planning, partnership, and creativity. Oh, yes, and time). A quarterly board meeting of four hours should be designed five to six weeks in advance so that you can deliver on the following:

- *Put on a Show.* Hey, if you want your audience to go out and sell "tickets," you put on a helluva good show. Every board meeting must bring the work to life and make every board member feel pride and privilege.

> Every board meeting must bring the work to life and make every board member feel pride and privilege.

- *Engage Them—All of What They Bring.* Chances are you have board members with vast experience across many industries. You need that and a board member expects to be asked to have an opportunity to strut that stuff. I've been working with an executive director who likes to present a new idea, as he says, *"Tied up nicely with a bow so they know he has* got it!*"* I suggest a different route that does not diminish the staff leader.

- Try this example on using two scripts.

  - *Script 1:* "We are exploring the acquisition of a smaller HIV/AIDS organization that will add a new program that will make the whole of what we do greater than the sum of its parts. We will add youth programs to our work, three strong staff members, and a cash reserve. We look forward to keeping you posted on this exciting development as our conversations continue."

  - *Script 2:* "We are exploring the acquisition of a smaller HIV/AIDS organization that will add a new program that will make the whole of what we do greater than the sum of its parts. There is an opportunity for us to add youth programs to our work, three strong staff members, and a cash reserve. As we continue to explore this new relationship, we would love for you to help us think through the questions we should be asking, the challenges you see, and how we might maximize this acquisition for marketing, fundraising, and to enhance the organization's brand."

Many E.D.s will avoid the second script for fear that the board will take ownership of the strategy. This is not my experience and a board chair with strong facilitator skills, along with planning each agenda item sent out ahead of time, should in fact result in the board feeling like a million bucks that you care what they think. And if you have the right folks on the board bus, you'll get smart questions and good ideas. And maybe someone will identify a resource they have for PR or something that would add real value.

How much better is that than a disengaged board member who leaves saying, *"The E.D. never let us into strategy and I had resources to bring to bear but I never felt they were valued"*?

- *The Inside Scoop:* Board members join to be part of a special club—to get the inside track on the issues in the sector. That's a big perk for board service. Don't forget that. So give the people what they want! A guest speaker? How about an expert in the field? Consider a foundation program officer who gives you money and knows the sector really well and how your organization fits into it. Be sure board members can ask questions.

- *Coffee Talk:* When I was a board member, I often felt I didn't get enough of the insights our E.D. had about the work. There was so much that was transactional on the agenda. In the case of this organization, the E.D. had a long tenure and insights I felt like others heard but not me. Which felt ironic. And frustrating. How about an "interview" with the E.D. to tease this out for folks?

- *Dinners:* You have to create a sense of cohesion on a board to build the kind of bonds, networking, and peer accountability that are critical to a high-functioning board. Board members will often balk at the idea of any programmatic element to such events.

- A few years back I worked with an LGBT family organization. Many board members had young children. I persuaded the E.D. and the board chair to have a chat over dessert with grown kids of LGBT parents—to offer a glimpse into the future. It was inspiring and the board members came to the boardroom the next morning enriched and motivated.

3. Regular Communications—the *Right* Kind

   Ask most board members about the emails they receive from the staff and they will tell you—"I cannot keep up with all the emails and every one of them asks me to invite someone to something, sell something, or find a silent auction item. I actually delete some of them without even reading them."

   Ask staff leaders and they will tell you, "I send the board an email with some great news about a large new gift we got and what do I get in return? Crickets!"

   Now you know why. The board member hit delete and didn't even read it.

   Again I say to board and staff leaders, take responsibility for what you communicate and how often and you stand a better chance of the information sticking.

- Reduce the number of emails. I speak from experience. Emails come from every which way and from board colleagues as well. And then my favorites are the folks who hit *reply all* resulting in 22 emails in my inbox that say simply, *"Great!"*

- Coordinate efforts in some fashion to bundle requests—it's just easier for a board member to look at a single email.

- Introduce an impact email. You might call it the "goose bump a week" email, but it's a story that you can arm every board member with that they can tell at the gym, the neighborhood barbeque when someone asks, *"Are you still on XYZ board? What's going on there?"* Give them a story they can tell in under a minute. And if you got a big gift, toss that in for good measure so the board member knows he is playing for a winning team that is doing great work and being recognized for it.

- This email, done correctly, is also an antidote for board inertia between meetings. Sometimes between meetings, board members have a tendency to disappear.

HOLDING THE BOARD ACCOUNTABLE

This is part of what should come up in those regular meetings I've suggested that board and staff leaders should have weekly. What's going on with the board? How is the committee work coming along? *Is* the committee work coming along? Does the E.D. need a particular board member to deliver on something she promised? Is a toxic board member sucking the life out of the person in charge of the annual gala?

If you have done a good job on making responsibilities clear, if you are enriching them so that their enthusiasm grows rather than weakens for the organization, if you have spent time talking about how to sell the organization (see Chapter 3 for the keys to that), then you can pat yourselves on the back. But, of course, there is more.

More? You are killin' me here, Joan!

Yes, more. And this is where the board chair takes the lead. The staff leader provides the intel, but the board members are corralled by the board chair. Are the board members you carefully selected actually delivering? And maybe more importantly (and frighteningly), are they behaving themselves?

And trust me. You will want to let people off the hook. I see it all the time. These board members—they are volunteers, after all. How can we expect them to fire on all their pistons?

HERE'S WHAT THEY SIGNED UP FOR

So a few tips for you as the board leader on managing the board:

1. Zero Tolerance for Bullying

There—I said it. Board members can abuse their power and, sadly, can be rude and nasty to staff members. I bet I get five emails a week from staff members who feel they are being treated inappropriately by board members. Granted, I have seen super-sensitive staff leaders who might hear something more harshly, but still. As a board chair, you should have some ground rules for board engagement with staff. I'm not suggesting that board members be kept from interacting with staff— some staff leaders ask for that and I find that excessive. But how about a simple rule?

> If you are angry or frustrated with a staff member about something, raise it with me (board chair) first. There is an unequal balance of power that makes the relationship tricky and will make the feedback feel particularly harsh.

And if your board member is just plain toxic (at board meetings and with staff), then the board chairs and staff leaders need to strategize about the best way to manage the person off.

2. Peer Accountability

Here's another ground rule an incoming chair can set.

> Let's work together so that the staff does not find themselves in the awkward and inappropriate role of nagging the board.

Can you imagine any of your fellow board members nagging their bosses endlessly to get what they need to do their jobs? The power balance is all wrong.

The most obvious area in which this plays out is with development. We'll talk more about this in Chapter 5, but here's what I see all the time: The person in charge of development reports to the E.D. and spends most of her time nagging the board to deliver on corporate gala sponsorships, invitations to a donor event, and so forth. So the development director is in the position of nagging her boss's boss.

It happens every single day in nonprofits everywhere but, considered in that light, it's just plain wrong. The board should set its own goals, push colleagues to make commitments, and follow up to ensure they deliver.

3. Board Self-Evaluation and Term Limits

I am an unabashed believer in term limits. On the positive side, it forces a board to consider a leadership pipeline and leads the recruitment committee to approach its work with real strategy and intention. In this case, it can be a mechanism to manage nonperformers or toxic board members out.

The vast majority of boards have no self-evaluation process in place. You would not accept that from your E.D. and how she or he manages the staff. It should be no different with the board.

PUT IT ALL TOGETHER AND WHAT HAVE YOU GOT?

Perhaps your answer is simply: "Absolutely no time to do anything else!" Please allow me to offer a different perspective.

I recently interviewed my friend Scott about nonprofit board service. He is a high-powered partner at a law firm and sits on three boards.

Is there a particular board of the three that you would consider high-functioning? Yes, he told me with no hesitation. I asked him to tease out the elements. He was happy to oblige.

- The mission of the organization is clear.
- There is no mistaking this organization from any other. I know what it does and why it is important. I can tell many stories about success. I can articulate the challenges and I have a sense of where we are headed.
- Everyone on the board is very passionate about the mission—to a person.
- There is almost a palpable tone of reverence for the work. People stretch because of the seriousness of their commitment. Enthusiasm is high and I am inspired to stretch.
- We hold ourselves accountable. Board members are expected to come prepared. Board members have been socialized to avoid wasting time with comments that are not well thought out. The board co-chairs understand their role to facilitate, to use the time well, and to ensure that all voices are heard. The meetings are well-planned. I never leave thinking that any of my time has been wasted.
- Board members are smart and real. Like many Type A board members, I pride myself on contributing in a thoughtful and strategic way. Thanks to the wisdom and expertise on this board, I often learn important things from my colleagues. Board members are universally genuine, real, interesting, and impressive.
- The board respects the staff. There is intense admiration for the work of the staff.

When you put it all together, that is what you could have. That is what your organization, your clients, the community you advocate for—*deserve*. Nothing less.

Am I suggesting that developing this leadership partnership is easy? Of course not. Remember: I am the one who believes that nonprofits are messy.

Am I suggesting that it will take an unbearable amount of time? No. I'm suggesting that it will take a lot more time *up front*. I work with many boards where we have to break bad habits. I'm suggesting that if the board chair and the E.D., when one or both are new, can sit down together and follow some of this actionable advice, together they can build the kind of board that really does exist. Like the one my friend Scott described.

That said, Scott offered a very important clue that takes us to the next chapter. You can have the finest group of board members assembled, but they cannot put their foot on the gas pedal if the mission is not clear and the vision for the future is either blurry, hard to articulate, or currently nonexistent.

Time to talk strategy.

"You want to triple your capacity without a strategic plan? Don't mind Charlie. My dog often finds things funny."

Chapter 4 The Key Is Not in the Answers. It's in the Questions.

Building Successful Strategies with Room for Innovation

THE POWER OF DELETING A WORD

Fingers crossed that the first few chapters have offered you new perspective on nonprofit leadership. Maybe you even took notes or sent a copy to a friend (this idea I like quite a bit). And then you turned the page, saw the word *strategy*, and fess up. You rolled your eyes a bit, right? Perhaps you are a board chair and know that the organization you lead doesn't have the kind of money necessary for the kind of strategy work you do in the private sector. Or you have an executive director who balks at the idea—too much work for a process that will unearth nothing new.

I wish more nonprofit leaders felt differently. I get business inquiries frequently. "We have to do a strategic plan" and it is said with all the enthusiasm I feel when I say to my wife, "We really need to do the laundry." Let's focus on the most important word in the sentence (no, not *laundry*): *plan*.

A few years back, I was working with a client that was tracking its progress against its strategic plan that had been approved by the board about eighteen months earlier. The staff found the plan utterly useless. The world of the senior staff revolved around a three-letter acronym: KPI. *Key performance indicator*. These are the granular activities that roll up into less granular activities that roll up into even less granular activities and then if you are really lucky (or patient), you find your way to some kind of overriding goal. Allow me to elaborate.

Let's say your overriding goal for the year in your area of the nonprofit is to "run a more effective office to support the program folks so that they can serve more clients." A KPI might be "purchase electric pencil sharpener to increase efficiency." Okay, I'm exaggerating here, but this is how the staff saw it. The staff began to see KPI not as a three-letter word but as a four letter one. Why? Because all anyone cared about was how many KPIs they could check off in the space between board meetings. It was like a bad game show.

And then at each board meeting, the board received an update. After all, the board must fulfill its core responsibility to approve and monitor the success of the organization's strategy. In this model, board members were bombarded with a long list of the successfully completed KPIs. Oh, one of the things I just love about this format is that there is typically a percentage completion rate next to each KPI. So board members may learn that the office manager is 78 percent completed with the pencil sharpener KPI. Makes you want to poke someone in the eye with a 78 percent sharpened pencil, doesn't it?

The point here is that the work became all about the *plan* and that, as a result, every single bit of enthusiasm about where the organization might be headed was lost, squashed, or both. My client lost sight of what President Dwight Eisenhower once said, "Plans are useless but planning is everything."

> Strategic planning can become all about the *plan* and as a result, every single bit of enthusiasm about where the organization might be headed may be lost, squashed, or both.

The folks at the Monitor Institute (www.monitorinstitute .com), an arm of Deloitte Consulting, have done a great deal of thinking and writing about how nonprofit organizations should approach strategy work, especially in a world that moves as quickly as ours does. In their article, published in the *Stanford Social Innovation Review: The Strategic Plan is* (sic) *Dead; Long Live Strategy*. They capture it well. "Instead of the old approach of 'making a plan and sticking to it, ...' we believe in '. . . setting a direction and testing to it,' treating the whole organization as a team that is experimenting its way to success."

I'm with President Eisenhower and the smart folks at the Monitor Institute. It's time to throw the word *plan* overboard and begin to think about strategic planning differently.

It's time to stop engaging planning efforts that suck the life out of people. The irony is too much for me. A great strategy conversation should breathe life into the organization and its stakeholders.

> It's time to stop engaging in planning efforts that suck the life out of people.

THE POWER OF INQUIRY

I never rolled my eyes when I was in strategic planning mode as an executive director and it's not because I am a strategy geek.

It's because I am a problem solver. I love to think through knots that need to be untangled. I love to debate options with smart and diverse folks. During my tenure as an executive director, I had smart senior staff that knew the tough questions to ask and I believe I created an environment in which it was safe to ask them. I also had a critical mass of smart and committed board members that allowed for the kind of robust conversation that most of them had joined the board to be a part of in the first place.

And I'm not talking about questions that land in the tactical space. You have to ask the *right* questions, and these are often the questions one level underneath your initial questions.

Here's what I mean. For example: *How do we increase the number of students in our upper school and retain them?* This is *a* question but not *the* question. *The* question might be, *"Given that our best efforts to market and recruit have not succeeded, and we can't get sufficient enrollment to be profitable, and our attrition numbers are well above average, what radical, innovative decisions could we make to solve this? And closing the upper school should be a decision to explore."*

Or this one from a nonprofit journalism organization that creates long-form journalism offered to mainstream news outlets for greatest impact and reach: *"How do we drive more traffic to our website?"* Isn't the real question: *"What is our website strategy? What do we need the website to do for us? Our site will never have the reach of* The New York Times, *so if our mission is about reach, about public education, what is our web presence really about?"*

The really swell thing about strategy work that begins with unearthing the important strategic questions is that there is only *one thing* you need to do it really, really well. Were you thinking I was going to say, "A blank check"? Sure, could you hire someone to help you figure out those questions? Absolutely. Would you wind up with a solid set of questions? And could that same person help you navigate the discussions and either provide or direct you to the resources that will give you what you need to answer them? Indeed.

So what is that one thing you really need? Guts.

People talk about innovation all the time. It's a key buzzword in our society. And we often focus on the outcomes of innovation. But where are its origins? The origins are found in a smart, dedicated staff and board, who the knots in an organization and are bold enough to ask the tough questions.

> People talk about innovation . . . But where are its origins? The origins are found in a smart, dedicated staff and board, who observe the knots in an organization and are bold enough to ask the tough questions.

WE'RE ALL IN THIS TOGETHER

I've known a few E.D.s in my day who didn't exactly respect their board when it came to designing the future of their organization. Okay, more than a few. The folks that feel that way, end up with a strategy that is exactly what they want, but it:

- Doesn't have the benefit of the good thinking of smart people outside the staff.
- Is rubber-stamped by the board who approved it but did not have a voice in it, doesn't own it, and is not invested in its success.

There's another big problem with this approach. It's actually not your job. Well, not your job alone, anyway. The development and approval of the strategy is a responsibility that ultimately rests with the board.

> The development and approval of the strategy is a responsibility that ultimately rests with the board.

So how does an E.D. juggle what she or he feels is a serious imbalance between board and staff around the knowledge and understanding of the organization, its future challenges, and its opportunities?

Wait. What? A serious imbalance? Let's start with the problem embedded in that feeling. There should not *be* a serious imbalance. Remember:

1. The E.D. is not the lone juggler. She or he has a partner in the board chair (time to reread Chapter 3?). It can be so easy to forget, though, right? And it can be so much easier to just do it yourself, right? Wrong. At least not in the long run.
2. Why *doesn't* your board have the knowledge and understanding? Isn't it the job of the board and staff leaders to ensure that meetings and communications are designed in such a way that board members can engage in rich, robust strategic conversations?
3. You may just not have the right board members. I did mention something earlier about how important that is. This is one of the places where a great diverse board really gets to shine.

I Don't Have All the Right Ingredients!

So let's get real for a minute. Suppose you haven't fed your board so they can really deliver for the organization on strategic conversations. Maybe you have a weak board chair or a weak executive director. Maybe you have all the wrong board members. Should you move forward with a strategic process or should you delay? My advice? If at least one of your leaders is strong, you have some strong staff, and a few good board members, you're good to go. And most organizations have that much. One more suggestion: This is a fantastic opportunity to engage a few smart outside folks—one or two nonboard members can add real value. What about a key donor who is not interested in board service but happens to work at a strategy consulting firm?

So get your best and brightest to say yes and build the team creatively if you need to. Then the two leaders of the organization will be able to lead the strongest possible team to create the strongest strategy for the organization you all care deeply about.

START AT THE VERY BEGINNING

The first question to ask as part of a strategy initiative is the same regardless of your nonprofit: *Does our mission statement continue to reflect who we serve, what we do, and the intended impact?*

You have to start here because the discussion that follows is the perfect kickoff to any good strategic inquiry. Your strategy is the essence of your organization. It has to be right and in a surprising number of cases, it isn't. And in an equally surprising number of cases, a strategic plan can miss this part of the process altogether. For nearly, a decade I ran the Gay and Lesbian Alliance Against Defamation (GLAAD). When it was founded in 1985 by a small group of attorneys, its mission statement read: *GLAAD works to promote positive portrayals of gay and lesbian people in the media as a means to end homophobia and discrimination based on sexual orientation.* In 1985, this made all the sense in the world. The organization was founded in reaction to the homophobic coverage of AIDS in national and local news coverage and to films and TV shows that either omitted gays altogether or depicted them in a negative light—as deviant, unhappy, and unable to sustain any kind of lasting relationship.

By 1995, the organization's work had expanded and the group of stakeholders—volunteers, donors, and board members—had grown and diversified. The GLAAD family now included men and women affiliated with the media and so when the group began to update its strategy, the mission statement raised a fundamental strategic question: *Can we legitimately ask the media to cover the gay community only in a* positive *light?* With media executives now at the table, the answer was a resounding "No." The job of the media is to be fair, accurate, and objective. While this led to many changes in strategy, the lead change was the mission statement: *GLAAD works to promote fair and accurate inclusion of the gay and lesbian community in all forms of media as a means to end homophobia and discrimination based on sexual orientation.*

So it all seems obvious, right? Maybe even straightforward? Maybe not. I was recently asked to help a board become more effective ambassadors for the work of that organization. I did my homework, was inspired, and happy to help. The organization was rooted in the Catholic tradition, providing shelter and job training for homeless adults and families in an urban setting. The work is important and Catholic parishes and schools serve as feeders for both the volunteers and the clients.

But my homework unearthed a fundamental strategic problem with the organization—a core strategic question that flies out at you just by reading the mission statement carefully. Here's the mission statement. See if you can see what I did:

Our organization provides hope for families—keeping them together and supporting their efforts to rebuild independent lives. We serve the Catholic and broader community, offering shelter, mental health services, and workforce development programs, addressing each client holistically and offering them hope and a brighter future.

Look closely for the big strategic question screaming out of this mission statement. I summed it up toward the end of the training when I asked the board how long they worked on the development of this mission statement. I took a guess that it was a protracted, perhaps even difficult conversation. They asked me how I knew. Instead of telling them, I asked another question: "How long did it take you to settle on the word *broader?*" *Forever,* they nearly shouted in unison. Bingo.

This wonderful organization had the need and the opportunity to answer one of its most significant strategic questions when it explored its mission statement in depth. Must you be committed to Catholicism to be eligible for their services? Some board members were adamant about this. Others not, so much. There clearly was not consensus on the board. The result? A mission statement that does not put a clear stake in the ground to answer a key question: *Whom do we serve?*

A MISSION SNIFF TEST

You don't have to save this test for the kickoff of the process to develop your organization's new strategy. Frankly, I think you should consider it as part of an annual check-up. That said, this is an excellent and easy way for an organization to explore the assets and strategic challenges of its mission statement with substantive context from those who know the organization best.

Feedback from external stakeholders is critical to any strategic inquiry, and when hired to do a comprehensive strategy for an organization (and an accompanying work plan), I rely heavily on qualitative information from stakeholder interviews. A key question we ask? *What do you understand the mission of XYZ organization to be,* and we capture their words verbatim. We may learn more from this one question than any other.

About two years ago, I was retained to work with a client and we began with 65 interviews. We captured 65 mission statements, including my favorite one: "They—um—I give up." When completed, we told the board and senior staff that we captured essentially over 50 *very different* mission statements. Pun intended here: Mission control, we have a problem. More on that client later—stay tuned for a happy ending.

Many organizations will not have the money (keep reading—I'm getting there) to hire someone to conduct interviews, and so my "sniff test" can do the trick. Let's assume that you are going to have a board or staff retreat to kick off the process. One month before, you give this assignment to every participant: Identify five people who are connected to the organization in some way—a colleague in the sector, a donor, an elected official, a reporter, a volunteer, a ticket buyer to an event—and email those names and their affiliations to staff member Mary. Mary makes sure the list is representative and diverse and then sends everyone on his and her way. Each person reaches out to the five folks with this message:

We are embarking on a process to evaluate our current strategy and make changes as we see fit and we can't do it without feedback from external folks close to the organization. I have just two simple questions for you:

1. What do you understand is the mission of our organization?
2. Can you describe a tangible success the organization has had in the last year? If yes, what was it? And why was it important?

Capture their answers verbatim. That's really important. Verbatim.

With a big organization, the info can be compiled and circulated before the retreat. If your organization is small, invest in large Post-its and have folks walk into the retreat surrounded by the answers—mission statements on one side and successes on the other. That will be all the context you really need to kick off a discussion about the big questions you have to answer to build an effective strategy for your organization, and you will do so with external feedback all around you (literally).

WHAT SUCCESS LOOKS LIKE

I mentioned earlier my client and the 50 different versions of the mission statement I heard during stakeholder interviews. I bet you're wondering how that all turned out.

We were hired to answer a question that on its surface appeared to be quite simple: *Can you help us find a path to sustainability?* If there is one thing I have learned about clients it is that the question I am asked to answer is infrequently the right question. You have to dig around and see just how messy things are and pretty quickly you are able to discern the *underlying* question. In the case of this organization, the CEO and founder wanted us to help her figure out how to raise more money. *Who else can we be asking? Is our development director strong enough? How do we find prospects?* If an organization is having trouble raising money, 99 percent of the time there is a systemic problem—mission, quality of service, reach, messaging, weak board—the list goes on.

It was clear that this organization needed a new strategy. And so we set off to help them create one.

With this client and others, we follow a certain recipe—many do. Whether you hire a big firm, a single individual, or have no resources and do it yourself, the steps are all basically the same.

Step 1: Assembling a Strategy Working Group

As I noted earlier, it takes a village to build a strategy. I won't work with a client that does not see value in engaging people who are connected to the organization in some way, internal or external. The strategy group generates names and compiles a list. This list is evaluated to ensure it is representative and diverse and then outreach begins—with a message that asks two questions. The first should capture an individual's perception of the organization's mission. The second should ask for an example of one of the organization's successes from the past year. See the example earlier in this chapter for specific wording if you need it. Document these answers word for word. You will need them for the next step.

With mission statements and the answers to these questions compiled, you will have what you need to begin a substantive discussion about the big questions you have to answer to build an effective strategy for your organization and you will do so with important external *feedback*.

Step 2: Checking Under the Hood

This is all about getting a three-dimensional look at the organization. Engage in analysis and interviews. Focus on fundraising strategy, financial statements and cash flow, and the org chart. And be sure to look at the competition and the sector in which the organization lives. Then interviews galore—internal and external. Learn about what's working and what's not. At the end of this step, like any good physical, the diagnostician sits down with the "patient" (board plus senior staff). We present our findings in the form of key questions.

Sometimes our clients are not always clear about this. If you spend a month or two asking questions, why do you not have answers? The simple answer is that organizational challenges typically stem from unanswered questions.

In the case of our nonprofit media client, there were significant questions to answer:

1. Should you remain a nonprofit organization or become a production company?
2. Is this organization wed to its commitment to public media (a distribution channel that is limiting in terms of sheer numbers and demographics)?
3. Is the public media audience the one you want to reach? Or do you want others to know and hear those stories? If so, who are those others?

See why sustainability is an issue?

Step 3: Attacking the Big Strategic Questions

In this next phase, I spent a lot of time with the client and our strategy working group (board and staff a must). We met often, brainstormed, and together, figured out what other information we could use that would be helpful in answering the questions.

Actually, let me take that back—we identify information that would be helpful in shaping *possible* answers to the questions. In my world of strategy work, there are always different paths the organization can travel and the goal of the process is to explore several options to present. First of all, there is never just one answer and to present a single strategy gives the board no frame of reference. Second, you own the path when you have to intentionally select it from a short list. Think of it this way: When you go shopping for something to wear for a big occasion, do you buy the first thing you try on?

The other important part of this phase is testing. I like the Monitor Institute's philosophy, which I mentioned earlier: *treating the whole organization as a team that is experimenting its way to success.*

So, when we work with clients, we brainstorm ideas to test-drive a possible direction. In the case of this client, we developed a plan to pilot a podcast to determine if it might increase the organization's impact.

During this phase, the working group works. They have relationships that can get us information and propose ideas more quickly than we can. Also, we worked closely with the staff and built multiple organizational charts—each path demanded something different. And each of those charts had a different price tag.

With this public media client, we really focused on reach. We probed (maybe even lobbied) the client to look at the limiting nature of public media and to look at other forms of distribution. We knew that clarity and reach across platforms would drive dollars.

Four months of work—inside the organization, talking with media folks, and putting the working group to work paid off. Let me also say that the group was fully engaged and felt a real sense of ownership about the outcome. Folks raised their hand to have meetings and to spend extra time in their day to develop ideas to test and volunteered to execute them. Being a part of this group was not a burden. The work was exciting—it was not about how we were going to stay alive, but how were we going to come to life.

Step 4: Putting a Stake in the Ground

This step takes the form of a detailed board presentation outlining possible paths and the implications of each. But the work is about more than picking a path. It's about picking a path that the board can get behind, that the board leadership believes can attract the cream of the board crop, a path with a marketable vision that will enable the organization to build its fundraising capacity.

And we always circle back to the very beginning—to the mission statement. Our new strategy and vision for our client led to a new mission statement for the board to consider.

Today our client still faces challenges; I'm not gonna lie. But the transformation is impressive and gratifying.

The board, once a group of four that played follow the leader, is now leading. It's a group of 12 and there are real committees and everything! And the increased reach and impact has opened many more doors. There is now a major donor program. New institutional funders have been cultivated and have delivered. Donors are cultivated at newsroom events where young and dedicated staff members share stories about how stories come to be.

One last important note. Their strategy is an ongoing experiment. They are continually trying new things. The picture isn't perfectly rosy and that nonprofit is still messy. That's how it is with nonprofits.

BIG DREAMS, BIG CHALLENGES, AND SMALL (NO) BUDGET

You may be thinking, "Good for Joan's client. They received a grant from a supportive funder to bring her in. I just asked everyone to empty their pockets and we came up with $6.27 and a whole lot of lint." Are small nonprofits doomed to suboptimal strategies? Absolutely not.

Before assuming there is no money, try this. It worked with one client and another is waiting to hear.

Some strategy consultants will work with you to help secure funding. Try asking a consultant to put together a proposal with a clear situation analysis outlining why the strategy work is needed and why it is needed now. For example, I wrote a strategy proposal that looked at strategy and board-building (these are intrinsically tied together, of course) for a school for hearing-impaired kids. I made the case for urgency due to the upcoming retirement of the head of the school. The proposal is in front of a funder who has been continually generous. This strategy work will secure that investment by making sure that the organization has a strong North Star, that it addresses challenges with its revenue model, and that it has a strong board. These are the things an organization needs to have in place to recruit the best possible talent to lead the school in the years ahead. The money may or may not come through, but it's a strong, detailed proposal with a sense of urgency behind it.

If you come up short, there is a way to execute a smart and successful process inexpensively. Hire a good consultant on the cheap and build a strategy working group that is prepared to do very interesting work—that group essentially becomes the consultant's team, working under her or his guidance and direction. The consultant guides the efforts and facilitates the in-depth work of the team. Do it in the summer when things tend to be the quietest. Market participation in the group as an opportunity to have a real hand in building the future of the organization. This format can work with small, strategic initiatives and the development of a full organizational strategy.

I worked with a community center anxious to bring more women in the doors. We pulled together a terrific group of folks who brought the kinds of skills we needed on the team—a board member with a marketing background, a staff member who was a CFO, a program person who had recently surveyed visitors, and another staff member with terrific institutional memory that offered critical context. The E.D. positioned it in such a way that it felt like an honor to be asked (in fact, some were miffed they had not been asked). There was peer accountability about getting work done and the quality of work was very good. Was it as good as the product of a highly paid consultant? I say yes. What it lacked in quantitative input, it made up for qualitatively and, most importantly, the group owned it and marketed the hell out of it—both inside and outside the organization. I facilitated several sessions of the group and drove them toward the creation of a board presentation outlining several paths the community center could take along with a good development strategy for each.

You could extrapolate this model for a full organizational strategy. In this kind of model, it would be exceedingly helpful to have a board member recruit a friend of the organization who has a strategic planning background to participate. There will be lots to do and it's possible that a person like that could work in partnership with the strategy consultant to move the process forward.

And oh, by the way, don't forget to start the whole process off with the mission sniff test. That's how you cover your external stakeholder interviews without spending a ton of money.

TEN FINAL WORDS OF ADVICE—KEEP THEM HANDY

1. Don't start the process until everyone is on exactly the same page about what success looks like and what the final deliverables will be.

2. Organizations typically can't afford to have the consultant stick around to create annual goals for each department. This may seem obvious, but don't forget to do this. I have one client that hired a big firm to develop a strategy for what the organization will look like in four years. There was not a document to be found that outlined the HOW! It's all well and good to build the WHAT and the WHY, but you need the HOW.

3. Before you begin to think about the new, think about the current. Are you sufficiently resourced to do all the things you do *today*? At GLAAD, our strategy included increased development horsepower to raise money to "right size"—to make sure we had the financial resources to do what we *were* already doing.

4. A strategy that excludes a meaningful change in the board to complement the strategy is incomplete and likely to fail.

5. The key ambassadors of the organization should be able to summarize the strategy and where you are headed in a few compelling sentences, inviting investment in the future. Your strategy should get people at hello. (See Chapter 3 if a refresher is necessary.)

6. I'll take Number 5 one step further. Build a compelling strategy and you can secure multiyear gifts. These are my very favorite kinds of gifts.

7. A plan that leaves the elephant in the middle of the room may succeed in the short run but the challenge will continue to haunt you.

8. If you are lucky enough to have a cash reserve, have a conversation about innovation and risk. As a donor, I'm all for

financial stability but also admire an organization that takes a smart risk in the service of greater impact.

9. If your answer to the question, "So what is your strategy for the next three years?" is something like "We are going to stay the course and grow by 15 percent," go back to the drawing board. First, the statement is an oxymoron. Staying the course won't generate new revenue. And increased revenue is not a strategy. It's an outcome of a strategy.

10. Ever heard this Stephen Covey quote? "The main thing is to keep the main thing the main thing." Repeat that mantra as you devise ways to monitor and evaluate the success of your work and as you consider how to provide information to your board.

And I'm thinkin' you may want to avoid KPIs.

"When you ask for donations, you will hear the word 'NO' a lot. I thought this might be helpful."

Chapter 5   You Can Do This

Fundraising is about an invitation to join you in the remarkable work you do. It's about building relationships that last.

Dear Joan:

I'm applying for my dream job. I've always wanted to run my own nonprofit. But there is a flag on the field. I've not done much (any?) fundraising? How can I persuade the board to take a leap of faith? I know I care deeply enough about this organization to ask anyone to do anything for it. But a check would be a new thing for me.

Signed,
Dreaming About My Dream Job

Dear Dreamy:

First, congratulations on getting an interview for the "dream gig." Remember, the search committee or headhunter must see some skills and attributes in you that have brought you this close. So relax a bit and start thinking about how to message your past experience to fit the situation. In fact, I actually like your line *"I care deeply enough about this organization to do anything for it."* As a search committee member, I'd be impressed.

But you'll need to dig deeper and broader. I want you to think about the kind of person you are, your level of commitment and passion for the issues that matter to you and how you have translated that into action.

I speak from experience. I was one of the final two candidates for an executive director position at GLAAD. I won't bury the lead. The other finalist had many things I did not. Tons of community experience, significant gravitas, and lots of fundraising experience. As Charlie Brown might have said, I felt like I had "a rock." Not entirely fair. I was passionate, a strong communicator, a relationship builder, and I had experience in the sector in which GLAAD lived—the media.

When the question about my fundraising experience came, I was ready. I thought—they are going to buy this or laugh me right out of the conference room. First I told them that I made the pitch for the Annual Fund at my kids' school. Parents said they came to hear my speeches whether they gave or not (I left that last part out). I had parents weeping, signing contracts in the moment and, yes, I'm guessing my remarks secured some gifts. But it was the next line I found to be the riskiest.

> In my current role at Showtime, I manage the joint venture between the company and Don King Productions (big boxing promoter, big hair, big personality, and big questions about his ethics). Every quarter, I sit with Don and work to extract money from him that he owes Showtime. Don and I have built a relationship that results in my

success. So here's what I figure: If I can secure funds from a person not interested in parting with them and who would be happy to walk down the street to HBO, I'm thinking you could put me in front of a donor anxious to hear how the work of GLAAD is changing hearts and minds, and ultimately laws, I should be really good at that.

Did they buy it? Were they impressed at my creativity (or my chutzpah)? I never asked. It didn't matter. I was offered a brand new low-paying job and never felt luckier in my life.

Until I sat with the director of finance and realized we had $360 in the bank. And $250,000 in aging (ancient) accounts payable. Oh, and then we had 18 staff members expecting paychecks (including myself).

And thus, on my first day of work, I realized that it was time to deliver on the promise—to put my hypothesis to the test. The leap of faith the board took on me paid off for the organization, the gay rights movement, and certainly for me personally. I did it. I raised a great deal of money that made a great deal of difference.

And you can do this, too. And I'm not just talking to E.D.s and development directors. I'm talking to board members. In fact, I *have* to be talking to all of you.

Fundraising is a team sport. Board chairs and staff leaders must lead in partnership to bring the two most powerful organizational engines together to identify resources for the important work of your organization.

And when I talk about fundraising, I need to clarify something; I'm talking about a direct conversation with an individual in which you talk about the organization you care deeply enough about to work for in either a paid (staff) or unpaid (board) capacity and say with clarity, *"Would you consider joining me in*

> Would you consider joining me in making a contribution to the organization in the amount of X?

making a contribution to the organization in the amount of X?" (P.S. Event tickets do not count—more on this in a bit.)

Okay, time to 'fess up. Some board members have never uttered these specific words. You've persuaded friends to join you at a fabulous event, maybe you have even sent an email to 10 friends to ask . . . maybe. And how many of you E.D.s and development directors have actually made the ask. Something specific. Not like, *"We'd love for you to get more involved."* (I see heads hanging low.)

I JUST CAN'T

Why not? You care deeply and you give time or treasure or both. Well there are many answers that range from "I don't have the information I need from the staff" to "I don't have enough time" to "I don't know any rich people" (more on this later as well).

I hear these all the time and we'll address some of these as we travel together through this chapter but I want to dive into the two I hear the most that just slay me every single time I hear them.

I'm currently educating a newly formed board about fundraising. I ask board members to write down one word that comes to mind when they think about sitting in front of a donor and asking for an outright gift. I shuffle the cards and have board members read each other's cards. The answers are always predictable. I'll see "nervous" or "unprepared" and occasionally I'll see "willing." But I will always see the word "terrifying."

FIGURE 5.1   Now *this* is what I call "terrifying!"

FUNDRAISING IS "TERRIFYING"?

Grown men and women, often with big jobs, responsible for large budgets and managing a team of people.

Terrifying. To put this word in perspective, I am kind to them and encourage them to think about the word *terrifying*. I suggest it be reserved for really big things. And then I tell them what *terrifying* looks like to me (see Figure 5.1).

I have the kind of demeanor that leads folks to laugh and not be insulted when this slide appears. They laugh. They get it. It puts the word in context.

MY FRIENDS WILL BE MAD AT ME

This translates into one of two things: (1) It feels really awkward or (2) Then they will ask *me* for money.

Again, we are talking about grown men and women, afraid their friends will be mad at them or (gasp!) that their friends may also have causes they care about!

Isn't it remarkable the kind of power money has over people? I try not to let it get me down but I am confident that if we had a healthier relationship to money, more nonprofits would have great development staff and first-rate board members and all the causes we all care about would move further down the field.

YES YOU CAN

This leads me to the three most important reasons that you can do it.

Number One Reason You Can Do It: It's Your Job!

For staff, this one is simple. As an executive director or a development director, this is what you were hired to do. If you find yourself at your desk for most of the day and look ahead to next month's calendar and don't see donor meetings (lots of them)—either stewardship or renewals or upgrades— you are not doing your job. Yes, yes, I know there is data to enter/manage/correct and upcoming events and "Save the Date" cards to get out. But this can't happen at the expense of personal interaction with donors and prospects.

As for board members, I'm going to let you slightly off the hook. Many, many organizations are so hungry for your board service that they are not as forthcoming about the fundraising obligation as they should be. They might scare you off, right? After all, fundraising can be terrifying. So it *is* possible that the responsibility was not made clear. And, by the way, this is a key reason that board members find fundraising challenging.

Number Two Reason You Can Do It: Money = Programs

A funny thing can happen to a board member when it comes to fundraising. It feels like an uncomfortable (dare I say *icky?*) task. Like she is being asked to sell an old broken chair to her next-door neighbor. Snap out of it! You are asking for money to support critical work that you care so much about that you chose to serve on the organization's board.

> You are asking for money to support critical work that you care so much about that you chose to serve on the organization's board.

Why don't you try this during the next budget cycle?

Let's have the staff build the budget that included the things they really needed rather than the items that fit into a flat budget?

Next, create the revenue budget you feel is realistic. Okay, now here's where it gets fun.

Before the numbers go anywhere near the board, prioritize and do the painstaking task of cutting critical and important items because you can't raise enough money. Maybe you decide to increase the revenue numbers slightly but you wind up with a list that we should just call "The *Not-a-Wish* List."

Before the finance committee starts nitpicking the numbers as they should, put this item on the agenda for the board meeting before you approve the budget: "Lessons Learned During Budgeting Process." Try to allow for 90 minutes of discussion. In this exercise, E.D. presents "The *Not-a-Wish* list." Make it clear and simple and powerful. Maybe just one page. With dollar amounts tied to each big item. And don't forget to total it.

So what is the purpose of this exercise? So many executive director clients of mine marvel at how quickly budgets get passed at board meetings. No one seems to ask questions, they tell me.

The finance committee can ask good questions but the budget is pretty neat and tidy by the time it hits them.

This exercise brings to life a reasonable list of program-related work, or work critical to doing that program work, that is *not* in the budget at all. It struck me the other day when I was talking a client who runs a $7 million organization and helping him with time management. *"Does your board realize that you don't have an assistant?"* Nope. Not a clue.

What if these things were on a list and presented and discussed? I think that if you have a good, solid board, there are two possible outcomes. The home run outcome? The board is horrified and establishes its own fundraising goal, commits to it, and instructs the finance committee to increase the revenue line by that amount and something important gets added back in. The other outcome is more fundamental. Your board (and development staff if you are lucky to have one) will see right there in front of them that money = programs. You move from a discussion of "this is what we can do because this is what we can afford" to a discussion of what is possible with greater resources.

And my hypothesis is that if you then follow that up with a discussion/workshop/training on the art and science of fundraising, your board will be exponentially engaged.

Number Three Reason You Can Do It: It Makes People Feel Really Good to Give to Causes They Care About

There it is. The sentence I was told that turned me from a fundraising virgin to a joyful, exuberant, bold, and passionate fundraiser. I cared about the organization with every fiber of my being *and*, by asking for money, I could make someone really happy. Many people drawn to nonprofit work have "pleaser" personalities. And so I realized that fundraising was a twofer—I could give someone the opportunity to feel good and thus set off all my pleaser buttons! Win-win!

YES, YOU WILL SCREW IT UP

So there I was at my first fundraiser. A major donor event—a room full of $1,000+ prospects, a few board members—my development director has prepped me and, besides, I am just one of those people who comes prepared. I have an index card folded in my breast pocket. Handwritten notes like "Patrick O'Donnell, lawyer, $2,500 ask" and "Steven and Judy Gluckstern, thank you, major donors for 10 years."

I find Patrick, like the obedient E.D. I am. He is lovely and he seems very knowledgeable about the organization. But he is not looking at me. He is staring at my breast pocket. This goes on for an uncomfortably long time. Finally, I can't take it any longer. "Are you reading my pocket?" I ask sheepishly. He smiles. "Sure am." I have figured it out without looking. I have folded the card the wrong way. I try to compose myself. He is still smiling. I ask the obvious question. "So what does my pocket say?" He reads clearly. "Patrick should be a major donor."

I want to crawl into a dark, black hole, but this is a fancy apartment overlooking Central Park so I am kind of out of luck in the dark, black hole department. I can tell that Patrick is kind and I can also see a mischievous twinkle in his eye. The silence goes on and he says nothing. I am dying! He lets it go on just a little bit longer and then he laughed and said that he was impressed that I was so prepared and that I was well-informed, engaging, passionate about the work, and that I had expressed interest in him and who he was. "You are absolutely right. Patrick should be a major donor." And that night he became one.

I am realizing that I could write an entire chapter on my own fundraising mistakes and while that could be entertaining, I do need to maintain my credibility. With that said, here are a few more, each with a moral.

Don't ever assume that a person with capacity should give to your cause. I made that mistake once and the organization paid for it. I had finally secured a meeting with that big donor. What I thought were good sources told me that he hadn't given because he was too busy. He invited me to his glorious home in the Hollywood Hills. We got along well and then I used the word *should*. Something like "Given your credibility in the community, your name should be on our major donor list." All of a sudden, the air turned cold. (This is a figure of speech. The weather was glorious.) The meeting ended soon after and a few days later I received a letter from this donor with a modest check and an eloquent handwritten note admonishing me in a very pointed fashion. I held on to the letter and referenced it often.

As a P.S. regarding this same donor, do not assume that because someone has given wildly generously to your organization that they haven't been wildly generous to another organization (I should have done more homework before the meeting that got chilly). It turned out, during my college tours with my eldest daughter, we learned that this donor had spent millions to build a campus center at his alma mater. This donor gave to causes he cared deeply about. He was smart and strategic and I assumed otherwise. It was a very bad assumption on my part.

Then there was the time I asked someone for a gift that was much too low. How did I know? I asked for $10,000 and she was a person with significant capacity. We had agreed that this was a great place to start. Her response: "What the hell can you do with only $10,000?"

Hardly the response I expected. I decided to go the direct approach. "Clearly, I shot too low, eh?" I had already developed a rapport and humor was a part of that. She laughed. Then I answered her question—in great detail. But I am not one to leave funds on the table. So I continued. "Now let me tell you what we can do with $25,000." I was not done yet. "I tell you what—30 days from now we are having a major donor event at X house. I'd like you to come and I will consider it my personal challenge between now and then to make the case for you to consider a $25,000 gift. Then, you decide at the event the level that feels right for you." The donor liked everything about the idea. I did not stalk her but we worked strategically and yes, 30 days later, she gave $25,000 as part of an enormously successful fundraiser.

Fundraising is an art and a science. That means you will make mistakes. It also means that people will say no. And to those of us who are competitive Type A folks (those likely to join boards and apply for nonprofit leadership jobs), this can feel like failure— a screw-up.

> Fundraising is an art and a science. That means you will make mistakes. It also means that people will say no.

Just do your very best, work from the head and the heart, invite the prospect to join you in the remarkable work of the organization, bring that work to life with facts and stories and make an ask. Sometimes, it will feel like a home run ask and sometimes you will want to crawl into a big, dark hole. But after you ask, your job is done. You can and should assess and debrief the ask so that your skill improves. But the rest is up to the prospect.

CASE STUDY: GIRL SCOUTS AND THOSE DAMNED THIN MINTS

I selected a provocative title here for a reason and not because I have anything against the Girl Scouts (well, maybe just the

Weight Watchers membership fees). It's a fine organization that engages and empowers young girls. I probably should know more specifics given that I invest about $100 a year in cookies. Thus, my point.

Every spring, they come a-callin'. You salivate over the brochure and place your order. It's usually a very big order. You are delighted. So is the cute little girl in the green outfit with the sash. As I mentioned earlier, it makes people feel good to give money to causes they care about. But as the cute girl with the sash walks away, I realize that what's making me feel good is the idea of Thin Mints in my cupboard. And I know I am not alone in this. Come on. Be honest. Unless you have a Girl Scout in your family, *do you have any idea how the Girl Scouts will spend your money?*

I'm gonna go with "No" on that one. And how about this question: If the Girl Scouts came a callin' without cookies, would you make a donation? I think I know the answer to that one, too.

You see, for decades, we've all been trained. Make a donation and get a box of cookies. This is unhealthy. And I'm not just talking about the sweets. Okay, so we can't blame it all on the Girl Scouts but you must admit—they are an easy mark. They have trained us all into believing that people won't give to causes unless there are treats.

In my vernacular, "treats" are code. Code for tickets to events. Spend $100 or $250 and sit at my table with my friends—great networking, open bar, sometimes a few good silent auction items, maybe meet a new client or your next boss. Oh, and there is a rumor that a highly undervalued fabulous celebrity (yes, her show was canceled, but . . .) will be the MC—waiting for confirmation. Oh, and it's for a great cause—maybe I mentioned that I am on the board?

If you could tell your pal that there will be Thin Mints in the gift bag, it could put her over the top.

That's what I mean by "treats." Buy a ticket to this great event, have fun, and it will feel good because a portion of the profits will go to the worthy cause (that you happen to volunteer for, work for, or on whose board you serve). I have even heard folks say, *"Don't worry—there won't be a boring program—it's just fun."*

Perhaps I am exaggerating. But not by much. And, because this kind of fundraising is perceived to be the easiest and least stressful, and the kind of fundraiser where folks don't feel they are putting themselves out there personally, event fundraising is the go-to for the vast majority of nonprofits. *"At least I can get my fellow board members to sell a few tickets, or maybe even a table, to their company."*

Anything for that box of Samoas.

Now it's time to look at a different kind of fundraising solicitation. Here's an example of a pitch that I, as a board member of an organization, would make to a member of my community. To bring it to life, I'll use an organization that has personal relevance to me—The Ronald McDonald House. Let's imagine I am a new board member and I have a neighbor with some capacity—neither a pauper nor Mark Zuckerberg. My neighbor has kids.

Here goes.

> I recently joined the board of our local Ronald McDonald House. In many ways, the people there are extended family. In 1988, my niece Molly was born with serious medical issues. She was airlifted to a five-star hospital where she stayed for weeks and my brother's family needed more than a place to stay. They needed support, comfort, and a place they could call home. From the staff to the remarkable legion of volunteers there, my brother, his wife, and their

eldest daughter were treated like family. The love and kindness they were shown helped them through as much as the first-rate medical care. My brother's family went back and forth to RMH many times during Molly's all-too-short life. And as they become veterans themselves, they were able to provide support and comfort to new members of the RMH family. Since Molly's death, my brother's ex-wife and daughter Norah have volunteered regularly, and Norah, now a pediatrician, has been a speaker at numerous Sibling Days, offering hope and the kind of care to siblings that comes with having stood in their shoes.

RMH has a waiting list and is looking to acquire new space down the road from its current facility. We are looking for support to increase our capacity to help more families. I'm not sure if you know, but the McDonald's Corporation covers only 10 percent of our costs. And our families stay with us for free. Since my niece passed away in 1994, I have been a donor here. Would you consider joining me today with a $500 gift?

Now let's say that the same Ronald McDonald House was having an annual gala and that the child of a celebrity spent time there. It's a great charity and the room will be filled with elected officials, key business folks—a great room to be in. Tickets are $500.

So riddle me this. Are both $500 gifts equivalent?

Absolutely not. Let's look at the two asks and diagnose:

The Event Ask

- The $500 gift to the gala costs the organization something. A solid special event will spend 30 percent on every dollar it raises. Without calculating staff time, venue, meals, and so forth. So the gift is really $350 (and less if you factored in staff time).

- The gala ticket is a transactional gift. I pay $500 and I get stuff. Maybe an interesting celebrity, maybe a handful of business cards. Hopefully, I don't talk through the program and I hear something about the good work of the RMH.

> The gala ticket is a trans-actional gift.

- Can a gala ticket lead to something different and more? You bet. I am not suggesting that events not be a part of your revenue strategy. I'm suggesting that they have to be part of a larger invitation strategy—inviting people to move closer and closer to your organization.

- Revenue from ticket sales to an event is among your riskiest dollars. What if my friend is out of town next year? What if something happens and the event is canceled?

- Lastly, an event ticket ask is transactional and you do not have to put yourself on the line. You are selling a fun event that will be of benefit to your neighbor. You are not sharing in some fashion why this organization is meaningful to you and why you love it so much that you are willing to ask folks to join you in making an annual gift.

The Individual Ask

- As I mentioned earlier, you are talking about money—voluntary charitable giving. Even those of us with lots of experience get anxious. It's so much easier if you are selling those cookies.

- Every single cent of that $500 gift you get goes right to the bottom line. Unless you paid for the coffee. It is the most efficient way to raise funds.

- This is your least vulnerable revenue line. Your neighbor is not buying a ticket to an event; she is investing in the future of RMH and its ability to serve more kids and families like mine.

- You have the opportunity to talk about what the organization means to you and to tell a story about why it is meaningful to you. With an event ask, you are selling the open bar and the B-list celeb.
- This is an easily renewable gift next year and is not contingent on an event or its success. I just need to stay in touch with you throughout the year (two or three times when I am not asking for a renewal). If I can get you to the house to work one night with me as a volunteer, even better. That is the kind of engagement that leads to gift upgrades and greater participation by the check writer.

What is the big takeaway here? Event fundraising takes fundraisers off the hook. They believe they are building the road toward sustainability. But it ain't so. I'm not suggesting that they don't play an integral part of your fundraising strategy. But I cannot tell you how many organizations are *all* about events. I had one client with a $1.2 million budget. *All* of it came from events except for a sizable gift from the founder and now board chair (don't get me started on the complexity of this).

Or how about the conversations I mediate between staff and board when a board member from Cincinnati says it's time for a gala there. *"I can get the mayor there!"* she proclaims. Is there staff in Cincinnati? Uh, no. Is there current program work to point to that can be used for a fundraising opportunity? If yes, is a gala the only way to capitalize on that? Uh, no. How about getting a person of note in that city to host and underwrite an event at her home, invite the mayor as a special guest, and make a pitch for individual gifts? Any idea how much easier that is for a small or even a large organization than a gala?

Here's why I feel all this is so important. A thriving non-profit has a strong base of individual giving support—folks who believe deeply in the mission, who believe deeply that your organization is effective and impactful; folks who hear from the organization during varying points of the year so that they know their money is being invested wisely; people who feel as if they are really an integral part of the organization and its successes and who feel a deep sense of commitment to and urgency about the work.

> A thriving nonprofit has a strong base of individual giving support

You can build this from events if you are intentional. But the most effective organizations focus on individuals—who give at small and large levels, those who manage the purse strings at foundations. They identify folks, invite them in, steward them, are curious about who they are and what they care about, and draw them into the organization's family in a strategic and organic way.

And this kind of organization has done two things very effectively:

1. The board enthusiastically accepts its responsibility to raise money and monitor its success.
2. There is a strong culture of fundraising in your organiza- tion—from the person who answers the hotline to the administrative staff to the program staff to every member of the board.

Yes, I did actually say the two things a moment ago and I mean them. I believe that an organization's board can be enthusiastic about fundraising and that there are strategies for working to ensure that every member of the organization recognizes that fundraising is and must be a team sport.

HOW CAN THE BOARD TAKE THE LEAD ON FUNDRAISING?

You are skeptical. I know. That's never how it works, right? Staff nags. Some board members are rock stars and for others, you knock and no one is home. But the reason it doesn't work may be because the board recruitment committee never talked about the fundraising obligation (or more likely said something highly complimentary about how well the staff fundraises) but there is something else that needs to shift: The board needs to *own* its fundraising obligation. It must *lead* and not follow. It must be *proactive* and not put staff in the position to *nag*.

Think about that for a minute. The staff essentially works for the board. Of course, earlier in Chapter 1, I made the argument that nonprofits have a unique, diffuse power structure. It is true that the power dynamics between board and staff have an element of hierarchy to them. So in that context, imagine how difficult and awkward it would be for you to have to nag your boss to do her job. The staff end up resenting the board for not holding up its end of the bargain and the board members don't appreciate being nagged. Not one little bit.

> Imagine how difficult and awkward it would be for you to have to nag your boss to do her job.

So we need to change the paradigm. And we start it with rethinking the charge of the board development (fundraising) committee. Quite a few boards don't have them at all—in fact, I have several clients who don't *believe* in them. *"If we identify a few folks who are on the development committee, every other board member will feel totally off the hook for fundraising."* In fact, this same E.D. actually vetoed the formation of a development committee for this very reason (yes, I know—the E.D. can veto the formation of a board committee—another one of those messy situations). Now I actually get this E.D.'s point and it could be seen as valid depending on the charge of the development committee.

Let me pose a few questions about your board development committee.

- As the lead staff person working with this committee, do you often feel like you work for the chair of the committee?
- Is the chair of the development committee an enthusiastic fundraiser?
- Is attendance good and engagement high at committee meetings?
- Do you spend more than 50 percent of each meeting talking about the upcoming special event?
- Does your development committee make any effort to promote board fundraising?

Typical answers:

- Yes—It seems that they believe their role is to supervise me.
- No—There was some serious arm-twisting about this role.
- No—I am asked to report out, people raise concerns about numbers that seem low and quite a few people are unable to stay for the entire meeting.
- OMG yes!
- No—Too busy nagging me for detailed reports to present at the next board meeting.

If your answers were typical, it's time for a change. More importantly, you will never develop a group of board members who are even close to enthusiastic about raising money.

The new paradigm for a board development committee is one in which the board takes ownership of its own efforts and the committee works to hold all board members accountable to make its very best efforts to secure new financial resources for the organization.

This is what I believe a board development committee should exist to do:

- *Provide Additional Reach*—The committee should be advocating that each board member explore her or his sphere of influence for folks who either can give or can lead to someone who can. The staff alone has insufficient horsepower to hit its revenue targets without the board engine.

- *Provide Peer Accountability*—This is where the dynamics really change. How different would your organization be if as part of your board orientation, the chair of the development committee handed out a two-page fundraising plan document and set time for the new board member, one member of the committee and the staff liaison to review the plan after being given a deadline to turn it in. The group could then help with staff to examine all the plans, create an overriding board goal, identify places where there were duplications, and so forth. You'll find a great sample fundraising plan here at www .joangarry.com/nonprofit-fundraising-plan-board/

- *Cheerlead and Advocate for Board Success*—Change the development reports at the board meetings and give shout outs to board members who have stood out. Advocate for talking points, trainings, whatever the board needs to fulfill its obligations.

- *Monitor and Share the Status of Efforts*—At each board meeting, the development chair should, in concert with the development staff person, share updates, and diagnose what is going well, what could be going better, and where the opportunities are going forward.

Let me be clear that this kind of role for a development committee will demand a strong staff liaison. This is another key board and staff partnership in the organization, one that is often imbued with tension and animosity. Not only does it not have to be that way, it can't be that way.

BUILDING A CULTURE OF FUNDRAISING IN YOUR ORGANIZATION

> Dear Joan,
>
> I run office admin for a nonprofit and I'm frustrated that things keep falling through the cracks. One of our programs is to provide rent subsidies and one person called and was terribly upset. The check had not arrived and the landlord was threatening eviction. We cut a new check and voided the old one but found the original one just sitting near the copy machine about a week later. Jeanne said it was just an oversight. I get that mistakes happen but I'm so furious. What should I do?
>
> Signed,
> No Room for Error

Why, you ask, have I included this in a chapter about fundraising in a section about building a culture of fundraising? Let me not hold you in suspense.

To build a culture of fundraising, you have to build a culture of "meaning." I have a number of clients who work to improve the profound flaws in the criminal justice system. I like to think that my work is excellent with all my clients but each client has "meaning" to a member of my team. In the case of criminal justice, one of our team members has a relative who was incarcerated. I think about Tim during the most mundane tasks of my work. The same with our work in the women's movement. I have two daughters. My teammate has a daughter who is nearly two and attends many staff meetings. The work we do is for her. And I like to think we go the extra step because of that sense of "meaning."

Let's suppose that the frustrated manager had a meeting every other week and took the admin staff through the list of clients. But it wasn't a list. There were pictures. And for each picture, each staff member read three sentences that outlined the circumstances that led to the client's need. Folks go back to their tasks.

Now, when Jeanne goes to copy that check, it is now more than a check. It's a story. It's an apartment. It's a gift. It's an opportunity. With that kind of meaning, it would be mighty hard to misplace the check.

> When Jeanne goes to copy that check, it is now more than a check. It's a story.

This is what I am talking about. The board chair and the E.D. must build a culture of meaning in the organization they lead. If it becomes about balance sheets and approving minutes and making copies, then your organization will be good but never great; effective but not inspired; and you will never raise the kind of dollars your clients need and deserve.

I suppose I could say that in an organization that has a culture of fundraising, every single person—staff, board, volunteers, and donors—bursting with pride that they are a part of this work and has at their disposal at least two or three stories they can tell with emotion and conviction. And when I say *everyone*, I mean *everyone*. Everyone with skin in the game—staff, volunteers, board members, and every one of your donors.

A board chair once described it this way: When you decide to become involved in a nonprofit, you must always be wearing your "organizational glasses." This means always being ready to share your enthusiasm about the remarkable staff, about the urgency, the need, and always talking and meeting people through your organization's lens. Might this person be a degree or two of separation from the lawyer we need for our board? Oh, the person I play racquetball with is a videographer for a foundation—how might I engage her? These "glasses" lead to resources of one sort or another. And when you create a culture of meaning, rooted in the fine art of storytelling, folks will be lining up for their "glasses."

Think back to the chapter about storytelling. I believe I may have mentioned that it is the key to fundraising. Here it is: If you can tell a compelling, articulate story (goose bumps are a huge plus) and yours is the voice of a person who cares deeply about the organization, a check is the organic result. Once more for emphasis:

Credible Messenger + Compelling Story = $$$

SAVING THE MOST IMPORTANT LESSON FOR LAST

Perhaps this has been a theme running through this chapter, but I felt it needed its own headline. The key that unlocks every door to a thriving organization with stakeholders who stay connected over the long haul is the value the organization places on building, cultivating, and stewarding relationships. And this is the work of every member of your nonprofit. Each and every one of you is not only an ambassador of the work of your organization, but also a champion and an advocate for the communities you serve. And in the most effective organizations, organizational ambassadors become a village of people who care about the cause and care about each other. And in the world of fundraising, the moment you start thinking of a donor as a check that hasn't been deposited or get annoyed that they are not returning your call, you risk falling out of the relationship with them that is necessary for being the best you can be.

The story I am about to tell you is true. When I tell it, I hardly believe it myself. It is the story of a village of staff and board that worked together to steward a donor. As you read the story, try to forget that the donor was so rich (how rich was he?) that his house had his own zip code.

It was the evening before GLAAD's big gala in San Francisco. We were an annual and sizable client of the hotel, so they treated me nicely. I was in a penthouse suite (courtesy of the hotel). It was beyond lovely. I invited board and staff up to the suite so that we could practice board meeting presentations (board meeting in the morning, fundraiser in the evening). We were working and enjoying one another's company. The hotel had wine and cheese sent up. (They liked us. They *really* liked us.) We worked; we laughed.

And then the phone rang. It was one of our biggest donors. He had not RSVP'd to the event but had just landed on the tarmac at the airport and was soon to head to the San Francisco hotel we were staying in. Now, when you have your own zip code, you are accustomed to the finest accommodations. And he expressed disappointment that the penthouse suite was occupied. That would be the penthouse suite we were all sitting in. I told him that I would call the front desk and see what I could do and promised to call him back.

There were no other penthouse suites. There was only one option. We had to get out of Dodge and fast. And we knew something else. We knew this donor well—we had a long-standing relationship with him. He would want his penthouse suite but under no circumstances would he ever want to impose on his friends at GLAAD who worked so hard for a cause he cared so deeply about. So it was clear that, not only did we have to get out in 15 minutes, but he could never know.

There was no time for housekeeping. We all became the housekeeping staff. My board chair folded towels and my staff threw leftover cheese into their briefcases. And my favorite: My board member went through all three bathrooms, tidied up, and folded all the ends of the toilet paper rolls into those lovely triangles. I packed my roller board and we raced from the suite down the hall and into the elevator. The suite was ready. Oh, did I mention it was nearly midnight?

We exited the elevator and somehow the donor missed seeing us as he and his small entourage entered the elevator. We had done it! I settled into my decidedly smaller room and crawled under the covers, so happy that we had taken care of our committed donor.

I was nearly asleep when the phone rang. It was the donor. *"You gave me your suite, didn't you?"* I could not read his voice and was dumbstruck. I tried to play dumb but he wasn't having it. *When I called the hotel looking for you, they put me through to extension 248. When I checked in, I ordered something to be sent up and noted the extension 248.*

I had been found out. And I still could not read him. Then he asked me to meet him in the lobby bar in 30 minutes. Did I have a choice? I figured that PJs were not quite the right attire for a 1:00 A.M. rendezvous in the hotel bar, so I made a quick change and headed downstairs.

And there he was. Still hard to read. I sat down. I definitely ordered a drink. I had not a clue what to expect. And then:

I have been a donor to dozens and dozens of organizations since I was fortunate enough to come into wealth. And no one—I mean no one—has ever been so kind to me before. I am treated like a human ATM. Organizations know nothing about me. I am just a rich guy with a checkbook. Not only were you kind, but you didn't attempt to exploit that kindness to reap some benefit from me—to use it as a chit that would help you the next time you approached me for a donation.

He went on. As if this wasn't good enough.

I am so moved by the kindness of your team and so impressed with the integrity you bring to this work, I'd like to make a one-time pledge of $3 million as my way of expressing my deep gratitude for what you do for our community and how you treat the people who matter to the organization.

Okay, the story is true and the $3 million was real, and the funds enabled us to be a first-class advocacy organization—one that my $3 million man was proud of.

A quick quiz to end this chapter. What is the takeaway from this story?

- This is a story about how to raise millions of dollars.
- I hate you. Why do you have a donor with his own zip code when I don't?
- You were just plain lucky and you know it.
- It takes a village of dedicated board and staff and an understanding that people come in three dimensions in order to be a successful fundraiser.

Not the toughest quiz you will ever take.

We were all in sync—never any question. Mr. Zip Code could never know. We just needed to do a nice thing, the right thing for a man who was generous year after year in supporting our work. That's it.

We were all in sync. One senior staffer threw melted brie in her brief case. My board chair made my bed. Another board member folded toilet paper. There was a sense of urgency but also a sense of joy. We raced through that suite laughing the entire time.

Another important note: Mr. Zip Code had already given us a generous gift for the year. This was not a means to an end. We just worked together on what turned out to be a pretty remarkable donor stewardship effort.

It's a crazy story, right? Actually, it's not at all. Maybe it is because of the magnitude of the gift he made. But as I said, the gift is not the point. The gift was emblematic of a donor who felt like the organization cared about him. The process of getting out of "Dodge" was illustrative of the board and staff's shared leadership and ownership of the relationship.

It's not terribly likely that you will encounter a situation quite like that. But the recipe of the success is an easy one to follow. Here are two simple things you can do to create a sustaining connection between your organization and the individuals who support your work.

- *Good Old-Fashioned Thank You Notes*—No emails. A note-card with an envelope and a stamp that goes out *the very same day* as your meeting. I'm not kidding. Have the envelope addressed before the meeting. Everything will be fresh in your mind and you can wish them well on their bunion surgery or include a picture of your dog (if she showed you hers!). A handwritten note that arrives fast is gold. Because it says you cared. Just like the Hallmark people say.

- *Board Members Assigned to Donors for Ongoing Stewardship*—My wife and I give to many organizations. And we often receive either standard direct mail updates or a quarterly newsletter before we are asked to renew. What if every board member received a bimonthly draft of an email to send to 10 assigned donors? The email was simple and included a very powerful story—not a list but a story of something that would not have happened without your organization. *No* invitation to anything. Just simply a story that ends with *"When you read this story, please take a great deal of pride. Your fingerprints are all over this and all the other great work we do every day."*

The email cannot appear to be canned in any way. It must be in the voice of the author. Make a personal reference so that it cannot be mistaken for an email blast. I promise you that a few folks will respond and say, "Thank you!" A few will say how much they appreciated the personal touch. And not a single one of them will feel ignored come renewal time.

As the chapter title indicates, *you can do this!* And you can because you are surrounded by teammates, because your love for the organization is greater than your anxiety about asking for money and because, if you were not a person who believed in the power of relationships, you'd be one of those people sitting on the sidelines.

I have been a proud major donor and a corporate sponsor. I have been a board member and an E.D. In each of these situations, it was a joy and a privilege to be "on the field"—meeting and talking with folks who cared enough about the world around them to engage at some level with the organization I represented.

Fundraising is in its simplest form an invitation to come off the bench and join a remarkable team on the field doing the most remarkable work.

"You say you think of your staff as family. Have you ever tried to fire your own kid?"

Chapter 6 Managing the Paid and the Unpaid

(Or, I Came to Change the World, Not Conduct Evaluations)

I imagine the board deliberations about my hire at GLAAD. "She has *never fundraised!* We have no money!" And then the other folks around the table, saying "But she came from corporate America and has a reputation as a stellar manager of people and businesses. She can *manage* us out of this."

Clearly, the management side of the board house won the day. And, frankly, they were not wrong. The organization had just completed a major "renovation," merging numerous chapters into one national organization. It was a management challenge, to say the least. And a particular challenge because I was a nonprofit management virgin.

Day One. I was told that my first order of business was to fire a young man named Jason Burlingame. Exhibit A was all I would need I was told. Jason had written a letter to the deputy director that bordered on offensive. He was arrogant, bold, and by all accounts, a most entitled young man in his first job out of college. In the land I had come from, his level of insubordination would not be tolerated. The hubris of this letter was stunning.

And, before I could reach any decision, my phone rang. His immediate supervisor, Julie. You might remember Julie from the introduction as "Heart Monitor Julie." That call (yet another item to put on the list of gifts Julie has given me through the years) introduced me to the world of nonprofit management. There was something different about it.

> Promise me you will talk to him before you fire him. Jason's frustration is most decidedly poorly expressed but it is rooted in passion. It is rooted in believing that in a non-profit, you trade a big fat payoff for a voice—a stake in the game—the opportunity to change some part of the world for the better. He had great ideas and no one was hearing him out. He took matters into his own hands, never showed me the letter, and let loose. Just talk to him.

I did what Julie suggested and after my first meeting with Jason, I knew I was no longer in Kansas. He was passionate beyond measure about the organization, deeply committed to the sector, and I realized, in that minute, that this would have to be the most important attribute in any hire I made. You can teach the basics of management, but it is way harder to light a fire in someone's belly. Managing passion would be the biggest challenge and the real opportunity of management in this new land.

> You can teach the basics of management, but it is way harder to light a fire in someone's belly.

I didn't fire Jason. I'm not sure who learned more in that first meeting. Jason had his diva moments in our eight years together and we were quick to call him out on them. But he delivered. His work was of the highest possible quality because his passion for our work led him to hold a very high standard for himself and his team.

After my meeting, I knew in my heart that when it came to managing people in the nonprofit sector, I should get myself ready. I was going to get as much if not more than I gave.

Fast-forward years later and I was offering strategic counsel to a nonprofit E.D. He too had come from corporate America in a most noble effort to run a research organization desperately seeking a cure for a catastrophic illness. I asked him about his senior team, not as workers but as people. I had a hunch and asked about their families. He knew nothing about them—not even their spouses' names. Not only did he not know their kids' names, he wasn't sure they had them. In that moment, I knew he was not cut out to run a nonprofit. He talked a lot about how much more money there was to raise (sales), his cash reserve, but when nudged to talk about the progress the researchers were making, there was data but no goose bumps. He seemed like he could manage the organization well—it was financially sound and even had a cash reserve. But he missed what I consider to be the key element in successful nonprofit management, whether you are managing a staff or board members.

MANAGING IN 3-D

I guarantee you that if you evaluate staff or board members who did not work out in your organization, there will be a pattern. Sure, there will be people who did not have the skills to do the job but that's not the pattern you will find. The majority of folks who don't work out have come for the wrong reason. Author Simon Sinek has a single lesson—it's all about the "why." And in recruiting board members and staff members, understanding their "why" is your biggest and most important job. And I'm not talking about this kind of "why" —*I want to build my skills as a CPA.* That doesn't count. The "why" must be clear, articulate, and passionate. Why this organization? Why this sector? Do you have skin in the game?

This is what corporate America misses far too often. Corporations should be looking for these things, too. Yet, far too often, they focus on the "what" and the "how" and as Simon Sinek so eloquently puts it, you have to "start with why."

I met with a student interested in a TV programming internship and she had several rounds of interviews with a company whose programming she knew inside and out and felt really passionate about. She stopped by my office to tell me that she didn't get the gig but that she *knew* she wanted to work there after college. *Every* person she spoke to was kind, interested in her, and smart. Really smart. Now *there* is a person you would hire, right? Listen to all those "whys." Far too often, both the hiring manager and the prospect are focused on the "what"— from the hiring manager perspective, it's all about *what* skills does the candidate bring and, for the prospect, *what* is the compensation and is there a year-end bonus?

In the nonprofit sector, it's not about a year-end bonus check because there isn't one. It's the lesson that Jason taught me in that first week. There *is* a bonus, but it's not money. I know what you are thinking—it's about changing the world, right? Yes, it's that but it's also something else.

It's about having a voice.

This is the management gift that the nonprofit sector gave to me and the biggest gift that the nonprofit sector has to offer corporate America. When you are in a position to manage folks and their success is measured in dollars, it's straightforward. I'm hardly suggesting that all managers are of the "command and control" variety—*Reach these very specific goals that we have set for you and you'll get a 20 percent bonus. Reach most and you'll get a 10 percent bonus.* But surely it is safe to say that much of corporate America operates from the top down in this way.

If reasonable increases and bonuses were off the table, corporate America would need a new model. And they would, could, and should turn to the nonprofit sector for such a model. But it requires a greater degree of investment in your board and staff. It may be more time consuming, more complex, and frankly, messier. But you can't beat the payoff.

HAVING A VOICE IN DECISION MAKING

Here's what a nonprofit staffer and board member want to feel: "Decisions are not being handed down to me. I believe my thoughts, insights, and opinions have real value in shaping decisions."

The reason this can be scary territory for managers is because it is fuzzy. If you ask for a point of view, what is the expectation the employee should have about what will happen to that point of view? How much weight will it carry? Will the employee feel valued as a result? Or is there a risk that the employee will feel devalued.

Read on.

> Dear Joan,
> So my boss talks the talk and at senior team meetings always describes his management style as collaborative. He

tells us that our voices matter in the decision-making process of the organization. It sounds good in concept until he asks you to give a certain issue some thought—that he wants your best thinking on how the organization should tackle it. I go away and give it my best thinking and return to tell him I think we should do X.

I provide all of my good thinking and then he says, "Why don't you go back and give it some more thought?"

I get it. X was not the correct answer. My job now is going away and coming back with Z—the answer my boss was looking for me to affirm.

Why is he bothering? Just tell me that we are doing Z—won't it just save a boatload of time? And besides, I won't feel like my voice is worthless.

Signed,

Feeling Voiceless

Here is what I would tell Voiceless:

There are three possibilities here. One is that your boss doesn't really care what you think and has already made up his mind. I so hope this isn't true—and frankly, if this is the case, he should not have even engaged in the sham of asking. Time to freshen up your resume? Another possibility is that your boss doesn't trust you and asked either to affirm his belief or to be surprised. Time to take a deep breath and ask some real questions, hoping for candor. The third option is that he doesn't really understand how to ensure that voices are heard in a way that makes a staff member feel valued win, lose, or draw.

Let's see if we can eliminate lack of understanding as an option at all. If a nonprofit manager can get this right, it can turn a group into a team. It can make decision making better, smarter, and richer.

Before walking through a few core elements, let's answer a key question: Is there ever a time when asking for input is *not* appropriate? My sense is that in nearly all cases, if you are surrounded by the right people, there is only upside in giving folks a voice. I'd say there may be two exceptions and really only one. First, if the issue is inconsequential. You can create a sense that you are indecisive if you ask for input about every little thing. Surely, the selection of a new copier is not something everyone needs to weigh in on. And remember, every minute you spend talking about getting input is one less minute you spend serving your community.

The second circumstance is if you have already made up your mind. With the exception of terminating an employee, I believe that if you find yourself in this circumstance, you have missed a step, a valuable step to engage the voices of key players on your team. But how do you get it right?

Let's say that you are the E.D. and you are hiring a new development director who will be a member of your senior staff. It falls under nonprofit best practices to hear the voices of two groups—the folks who will report to the development director and her or his new colleagues on the senior staff. It can be really hard.

1. *Did you get input before the interview process started?* This is a smart tactic for a host of reasons. You may have some idea of who you are looking for but your smart colleagues will offer you more perspective and they have a view you do not. Together, you can draw a fuller picture of the ideal candidate. So add this to an agenda of a senior staff meeting. Call a meeting of the development team (or talk to each one on one) and don't forget the board! Most senior positions will have interaction with the board and you might find it quite valuable to hear what your executive committee has to say—perhaps a debrief of the prior

staff member in the job—and anything they believe you might want to look for.

2. *Be wildly clear about where the final decision rests and what you are asking for.* So often folks are given the opportunity to "meet and greet" possible final candidates. I think we should eliminate that phrase from the nonprofit glossary. It means nothing. As an E.D. candidate, I had an "interview" with a preselected group of staff. It was called an "interview" and this group spoke with both final candidates. They had no idea what their authority was. Because they were not told anything other that *"We'd like to have a representative group of staff interview our final two candidates,"* they *assumed* it was an interview and that the collective vote carried weight as a *vote*. This group was aware of the financial straits of the organization and upon hearing that I had no fundraising experience, unanimously voted for the other candidate.

Just a few days later, the staff learned that I had been hired. Well, that went well, huh? They were furious and thought the board was out of its mind. The process of including them backfired completely. Here's what they should have told this group explicitly: *"This is not an interview. The word 'interview' presumes authority and in the case of the hiring of an executive director, this rests with the board. That said, we believe that it is important to take your input into consideration as we make our final decision. And after the process is complete, we'll circle back and to the best of our ability, share our decision rationale, especially if it is different from any input you have provided."*

The same would hold true in our example of an E.D. hiring a development director. I generally recommend getting input up front from those who will report to the new hire rather than a conversation for input late in the game. It can be hard to offer objective feedback about which of two candidates should be your new boss. Colleagues are another story. I believe that a meeting with final candidates with clear expectations set can offer you that view you do not have that could shape your final decision.

OWNERSHIP OF THE WORK

Author Daniel Pink, in his book *Drive*, writes that when it comes to being motivated at work, there are three things that really matter. Money is not one of them.

1. Autonomy
2. Mastery
3. Purpose

I agree with Pink but I believe there is a missing number four. Stay with me.

So in the nonprofit sector, we have number three covered, and as I mentioned earlier, if a staff or board member is not dripping with a sense of purpose, he or she should not be allowed on the bus or be escorted off at the next stop.

Let's talk about Pink's number one and number two before I share my friendly amendment. Mastery and autonomy are the core elements of ownership, a key part of this idea of having a voice. This is not about having a role in decision-making but about the staff or board member's ability to develop a sense of confidence about her skills to do the job and being given the autonomy (what I would characterize as a good length of rope) to use this mastery to move her work forward.

Here's how I see it: A great staff member or committee chair becomes great when given clear expectations and just the right amount of rope to feel a sense of ownership and is managed by someone who stays close but not too close, acting as mentor or boss.

This makes all the sense in the world, right? Yup. But when you unpack the aforementioned theory, you have a few obstacles unique to nonprofits that can really muck things up.

1. *Everything matters. A* lot. How can I possibly delegate when there is *no margin for error.* Here's another phrase that needs to be yanked out of the nonprofit glossary. There is no learning without error and there is no innovation without error. There is no sense of mastery without it. And if you don't delegate, there is no sense of ownership of the impact of the organization and that is what your staff and board signed up for. Otherwise, your board members can just buy a rubber stamp and your staff members can probably get paid more to work in another sector with an equal amount of autonomy (read: not much).

> There is no learning without error and there is no innovation without error.

2. *Many board and staff leaders have control issues.* But not everyone! Let me be clear. I have seen hundreds of board and staff leaders who do. They didn't get to the top by being nonchalant. They are drivers. Often intense. I have one client who delegated a project to a staff member; it was a total success and she later admitted she was furious at her staffer. Being the compassionate truth teller that I consider myself to be, I put my response in the form of a question: *"Do you think this might indicate some control issues?"*

Do you have a tendency to tell your staff the answer? Come on. Be truthful. You are very smart, driven, and feel a sense of urgency. Why beat around the bush? Tell them the answer and then have them go do it, right?

Wrong. This runs counter to the culture of mastery and autonomy you need to foster to motivate your staff to go above and beyond the call of duty.

Try these two techniques and I bet they will help.

1. The power of "might":

   Instead of directly leading someone to an answer, begin a sentence with a staff member or a board colleague with this phrase: *"You might want to think about . . ."* I also think of it as helping someone *"Try something on"* in response to some problem they are trying to solve. It offers a sense of ownership. It can even lead to a conversation about why someone *might not.*

2. Another good trick to build mastery and allow *you* to offer a longer rope:

   One day, Glennda, my lead programming person (today an executive director in her own right), came into my office with a knotty problem she was struggling with. She asked for my help. I asked her a simple question:

   What would you do if I weren't here—if the decision was entirely yours?

   With that, Glennda spoke for maybe five minutes, outlining the pros and cons of each different option. Without my saying a word, she reached a conclusion about how to resolve it. And then I spoke two more words: *Sounds good.* And, with that, Glennda left the office with her problem resolved.

   How did Glennda feel after leaving the office? Affirmed that she was gaining needed mastery and a sense of ownership. I did not tell Glennda what to do. I was just listening and thought her path was spot on. The conversation built trust, which led to longer rope.

THE MISSING PIECE: CLEARLY DEFINED ROLES AND GOALS

Roles

It's possible that Daniel Pink took this last one for granted but in the nonprofit space where many senior staff members wonder if they ever *had* a job description, a clearly defined role is mission critical. Literally. The key to the motivation you have for your work is mastery and autonomy. Mastery about what? Ownership of what?

> The key to the motivation you have for your work is mastery and autonomy. Mastery about what? Ownership of what?

I encourage new executive directors I work with to meet one on one with all staff within the first two weeks. Before the meeting, I suggest that staff be given a homework assignment. They are to pull out their job descriptions and review them. They are to assess what is on the job description that they actually don't do—maybe someone else does that now or it's been so long that the staff member forgot it was ever on the list. They are then to write down what they are responsible for that is not on the list. This becomes the central agenda item in this one-on-one meeting (after getting to know the staff member and her or his motivation, sense of job satisfaction, and the names of any pets he or she may have).

This is an excellent exercise and can be revelatory for both parties. People can't develop mastery in their work without a sense of clarity about the specific work that rests within their purview.

I mentioned earlier that the nonprofit world has lessons to offer the for-profit sector (three-dimensional management). The reverse is true as well. The discipline of developing clear job descriptions arrived with me from corporate America and has held me in good stead ever since.

Goals

Here's another tool in my corporate toolbox. Annual goals. And a shared understanding of what success looks like. To make it a more lively exercise for staff, I call it "The New Year's Eve List." It should be developed as part of a staff member's annual performance review. And for board committee chairs, it's a great way to start the calendar year. It's simple. Here's all there is to it.

Ask every everyone—employee, every board member, every department head or board committee chair, to imagine themselves sitting in front of a fire on New Year's Eve. Ask them to imagine turning to a spouse, a kid, a pet, or an imaginary friend. Reflect on the past year. You have a glass of something bubbly in one hand and a document (or laptop) in the other. You'll need the document you created the previous January as part of this exercise. It should be one page and should outline specific successes you want to be able to point to while staring into that fire. I also call this document the "5 to 10 Big Things"—the things you keep your eye on all year—that guide how you spend your time.

And yes, these big things should be the annual big things that should surface from that strategic planning process we spoke about earlier. These 5 to 10 things each year from all parties, if achieved, keep your feet firmly planted on the road to the strategic plan destination.

When I talk about "big things," here are the kinds of things I mean:

- Create a strategy for board recruitment, beginning with an ideal board matrix. Use this to add three to five new board members this calendar year.
- Work with the board chair to develop a new model for board orientation, meetings, and communications to heighten board engagement and enthusiasm in the work of the organization.
- Manage out two poor-performing staff members, and by Q4, hire a best-of-breed replacement for both positions.
- Increase the number of clients served by 15 percent.

Get the idea? Now you can see that there are "hows" and "whats" that fall under each of these goals, but I believe that all board and staff should have a "New Year's List" and it should rest near your computer on your desk. As you careen through your day, peek at the list. Or perhaps every Friday, take 10 minutes with your morning coffee and look back at the week that was. How did you spend your time? There are only 52 weeks in the year, so I'm hoping that you will feel that you kept your eye on the most important balls. If not, it's time to start thinking differently about how you are looking at the upcoming week. No lie: 52 weeks goes by really fast.

And, of course, board chairs should have a similar list. You don't want to spend a year as board chair and then not be able to point to 5 to 10 accomplishments that you can be proud of that moved the organization forward, and had a clear intersection with the E.D.'s New Year's Eve list.

Okay, so let's recap. Here's what I believe I just said. You need to manage in 3-D. You need to motivate folks by stirring their emotional connection to the work. Then you need to give them a voice, allow them to have a strong sense of autonomy and you need them to do all of this through the lens of very clear roles and very clear goals.

AND WHAT ABOUT THE NOT-PAIDS?

So the core question here is: Do the same basic management techniques apply to a volunteer? Is there a different set of rules for them?

I have been known to say that nonprofits are messy—for oh so many reasons. It's because the answers aren't simple. The answer here is "Yes, but. . . . "

Why is there a "but?" Remember the Type A control freak I was talking about just a moment ago? The nonprofit space has a disproportionate percentage of them. Changing the world or even some small part of it requires some of that Type A juice. No doubt.

Here's the "but." Far too often nonprofit leaders are biased against volunteers. Seems crazy, right? Folks who raised their hands to serve on your board, a fundraising committee, to chair an event, to work check-in at a conference—you would never be able to afford that person power in any of those organizational spheres. And yet, I hear many leaders besmirch the very people they cannot do without. Why?

The three most common complaints I hear:

1. *Volunteers are too much work.* I have to figure out what the heck they can do that is finite and requires little supervision. I am too busy—this is just more work.
2. *Volunteers are just not reliable.* I just can't count on 'em. I don't pay them, so who knows if they will even show up when I need them. I take the chance.
3. *My work needs to be perfect.* I cannot afford to let any balls drop—there's just too much at stake.

And I'm not just talking about folks handling coat check at your spring gala. Leaders often express these exact same concerns about the most important volunteers they have—their board members. I know an executive director who won't *let* board members fundraise on behalf of the organization. She says it's because she is concerned that it won't get done, but I don't buy it. She wants control of those relationships.

Yes, it can get this bad. And yes, I will be covering burnout and retention, so keep reading.

Nonprofits need volunteers. I'm not dismissing the concerns staff leaders raise about volunteers—they can be real. And as a staff leader, you need to be conscious of managing risk. The fact that they are not beholden to you through payroll makes things a bit different. Volunteers can flake out. True.

But does this lead us to a conclusion that different management techniques apply? Absolutely not. In fact, I think the challenges with volunteers come from treating them *differently*. With or without a paycheck, a manager or a board chair must place faith in the people at the table, create meaningful opportunities for them, and appreciate the hell out of them. Each of these cohorts made intentional decisions to join your organization. They raised their hands and said, "I want in." So no kvetching. Make it work.

Wait, you say, maybe I get this with the board, but other volunteers? Really? Who are you kidding, Joan? Working registration at your annual gala isn't meaningful. I beg to differ. It sure is if your most significant donor's name is missing from the list or a major donor is treated poorly.

It is your job as a board or staff leader to inject meaning into each activity—to place it in context. In my days at GLAAD, we were totally dependent on volunteers for our annual GLAAD Media Awards—for several years the Los Angeles event was held at the Dolby Theatre in Hollywood. We would always gather all the volunteers together before the event and I would join for a few minutes—not just to talk about how much money the event would raise but a bit about how this money would be invested by the organization. And then I would thank them endlessly. We had a first-rate volunteer manager who loved his volunteers and his eyes twinkled 24 hours a day. Volunteers felt appreciated. Actually, more than that. They felt lucky to be a part of the event, whether they were a celebrity escort or worked at the registration desk.

THE CLASH OF THE TYPE A's

As I noted earlier, three-dimensional management is core to success in a nonprofit. So, as you consider how a board should best be managed, let's look at those folks three dimensionally as well. And when you do, you'll see that staff leaders and board members are dispositional kindred spirits.

Board members arrive on the scene because they too are of the Type A variety. Otherwise, they would be on the sidelines, in the dugout, or at home watching the game on TV. In nearly all cases, board members are successful and ambitious at their jobs. They are very accustomed to getting A's on their book reports. They have either worked ridiculously hard to get to where they are or they are working ridiculously hard to get to where they want to go next. Folks who raise their hand for board service are accustomed to environments in which there is a clear path to success and they are driven to follow it. They will do what it takes—nights, weekends, you name it. And success brings money, stature, or some combination of both. Board members, for the most part, arrive as winners. They are accustomed to winning and doing what it takes to win.

And then they arrive to their first board meeting. The path to success is not always clear. And, more importantly, the path to an A-level board member feels overwhelming. After all, these folks have day jobs in which they are very successful (a core reason you recruited them to begin with). It is unrealistic for either the board member, the board chair, or the staff leader to think that these board members will be able to give 140 percent to board service when they are often well above 100 percent on their day jobs.

Okay, you think, I get that. Who's asking for 140 percent? I'd be happy with, like, 85 percent from my most promising board members. Isn't that okay?

My friend and former board member Dan taught me that the answer to that is, "Not always." Dan was one of my highest-performing board members. He was strategic and asked good questions at meetings. He identified corporate sponsorship dollars. He loved the work of our organization and was an eloquent ambassador. He gave generously. And then one day he resigned. I was flabbergasted.

Our conversation has stayed with me. *"I just never feel like I am doing enough."* Enough for whom? As an E.D., I thought he was doing plenty. In *my* mind, he was a great board member. But not in *his* mind. As a Type A high performer accustomed to A's, he felt unsuccessful with his B+ as a board member—and his grade was higher than 85 percent of my board. But that was not his frame of reference. He gauged his own performance in the context of what he was capable of doing if he dedicated more time (which he couldn't). He applied "day job" standards to a high-level volunteer gig.

I can think of no more important context for managing high-level volunteers than this. How you set the role up makes all the difference. Shaping the responsibilities, the committee leadership—all of it—in such a way that a board member feels success as she or he defines it. Not how you do.

Dan left my board because he was basically beating himself up about what he was not doing. I felt this exact same experience when I sat on a board. I spent so much time kicking myself for the calls I said I would make that I just didn't—I had no bandwidth. There was so much more I *could* have done. And yet I do know in my heart that I was a valuable board member and one of the higher performers.

So I have seen it and I have felt it myself. What are the implications? Being a Type A and managing Type A's requires finesse. It requires, in my mind, a high level of clarity, clear management of expectations, and, with board members, an extra dose of appreciation. I still feel that if I had been more apprecia-

> Managing Type A board members requires finesse and an extra dose of appreciation.

tive of what Dan felt was a B+ performance, he would have *felt* that it was closer to the high standard he set for himself.

I believe it requires a few other components that tie right into managing the paid folks as well. The meaning and purpose of your work should always be front and center. This is why I argue so vigorously for board meetings that give board members goose bumps. "Goose bumps" is code for me—code for that visceral emotional connection that makes people feel good in their core, that they are involved, and motivates them to do more.

One last piece that is vital to the management of nonprofit personnel resources. Esprit de corps. A sense that everyone is in the work together. The work isn't easy. Sometimes the work is painful when you have real opposition. Sometimes when the work is rooted in tragedy, it's heartbreaking. You must feel a sense of team. And I'm not talking about two teams—the paid team and the unpaid team. I'm talking about a team of one—one which everyone is working collectively in pursuit of your mission.

Before reaching this desired end state that offers everyone a piece of joy and privilege, there's one word we have to define.

Team.

GROUP, TEAM, OR FAMILY

Dear Joan,

I am the COO of a $4 million organization and the E.D. likes to say we are like a family. I think it sets up the wrong dynamic—the E.D. is a charismatic leader and people want to follow him. The staff looks up to him because of it. And when he reinforces the idea of "family," he presents himself like a father figure. People won't say no to him and as a "pleaser," he doesn't say no to new ideas we can't implement or afford. I think "family" is a problematic metaphor for a workplace, especially a nonprofit. Frankly, we don't all get along very well (like a family), which is kind of ironic. So we are not even a good team. What should we be striving for?

P.S. I have a real-life dysfunctional family of my very own, so it doesn't actually paint the most positive picture for me.

Signed,

We Are *Not* Fam-ah-lee (1979 song by Sister Sledge—I just googled it)

Dear Fam,

You are, in my opinion, spot on. Words matter. I have worked with organizations that use the word "family" regularly. *"We work together and we have a shared sense of where we want to go—we are family."* All you really have to do is think about the distinction between a boss and a parent and you get it. There are nonprofit leaders who take pleasure in being thought of as a parental figure but it's not healthy. I could write another page or two on this but let's just cut to the chase: A parent can't really fire his own kid. A nonprofit is a workplace and you can create a culture that is nurturing but a family it is not.

> A nonprofit is a workplace and you can create a culture that is nurturing but a family it is not.

The other word that gets tossed around *all the time* without any consideration of its true meeting is *team*. I see this word used most often to describe the collection of individuals who report to the executive director. The management *team*. Or the leadership *team*. And then I see them in action. If they were a group of kids in the sandbox, the sand would be flying, there would be tears and let's not even think about sharing. I see some of the singularly most uncivilized behavior in groups that call themselves *teams*.

For staff leaders who just start calling their direct reports a team, it's time to hit the pause button and determine whether you have done the work necessary to foster a team environment. Have you talked about what it means to be on a team? Or your expectations of individual and team behavior? In my experience, *team* is assumed. Ask any professional coach or general manager of a sports team how often they talk about team culture. I'm guessing often. Because you don't win without one.

And then there are boards. They often don't even aspire to be teams—they are lucky if they even know each other's names. Or what they do for a living. Or why they are on the board. The list goes on.

You don't get to call yourself a team if you don't do the work, if you don't understand what the word implies, and if you don't see the value in those implications. That said, if you build a team and the board or staff leaders hold folks accountable to the norms that come with being on a team, guess what? People feel supported, the impact of burnout is decreased, and retention skyrockets. Now if that isn't motivation to actually walk the walk when it comes to team building, I'm not sure what is.

Time for another messy thing. In the most effective nonprofit organization, there are a few key teams and they intersect.

- The entire staff must feel like a team (especially true if you run a small org).
- The individuals who report to the staff leader will be a team and will model that for the rest of the organization.
- The board will be a team.
- This last one is important: The senior leadership of the staff (ideally, a true team) will relate to the board (ideally, a true team) in a partnership that feels team-like.

Can I be honest? The interchangeable usage of the words *group* and *team* bugs me—big time. So now that you know that my soapbox is out and I'm standing firmly on top of it, allow me to continue.

Let's dissect the two words with a simple grid.

Working Group	Team
Strong, clearly focused leader	Shared leadership roles
Individual accountability	Individual and mutual accountability
The group's purpose is the same as the broader organization	Specific team purpose that the team itself delivers
Individual work-products	Collective work products
Runs efficient meetings	Encourages open-ended discussion and active-problem-solving meetings
Measures its effectiveness indirectly by its influence on others	Measures performance directly by assessing collective work products
Discusses, decides, and delegates	Discusses, decides, and does real work together

If you want to be a team (and I'm here to tell you that your clients and the community you serve *need* you to be one), those hats must get left at the door and everyone must enter the room wearing an organization hat. Decisions are made collaboratively, with open communication. Diverse perspective is welcome; so too is healthy conflict because the team knows that it can lead to creative problem solving. The end decision is what's best for the organization and richer for the discussion and the debate.

This is what you are going for. Senior staff, full staff, and the board. Did you look at that grid and read the paragraph it above and say, *"We are* so *not a team"*? Join the club.

Here's what needs to happen to even hope to turn your group into a team.

- Every single person needs to understand the difference between a *group* and a *team* and must aspire to move in the direction of *team*.
- The leader (board chair, staff leader, or department) has to articulate the need—the charge for this group. Why do we need to come together?
- The leader has to establish expectations of the values and behaviors expected of all team members.
- An investment must be made by all parties to welcome and introduce each new staff and board member so they arrive knowing and understanding the responsibility that comes with being a new member of the team.
- You need to make time to talk through all of this. It's not a small agenda item in an already packed tactical standing meeting.
- Because of item three, the leaders of wannabe teams have to carve out time for retreats.

And yes those retreats must include icebreakers (sorry to break it to you).

RETREATS ARE NONNEGOTIABLE

An effective nonprofit needs to work as a team. Building a team takes time. There is never time. You have to make time. Thus, retreats are nonnegotiable and can be, if designed well, invaluable.

Back in my corporate days, retreats *could be* valuable—we'd cover annual goals or something that would take a good amount of time—but truthfully, it was in corporate America that I learned the word *boondoggle*. This is a word for an activity that costs time and money with an outcome that calls into question the time and money invested. That was diplomatic, huh? There was this one corporate retreat that involved night golf. Glow in the dark balls and headlamps. And a bar and food just behind each green. I will never forget it. Actually, I take that back. There is quite a lot about that evening I don't remember. But I digress. Here's where I'm going: If we opened the dictionary and searched for *boondoggle,* we might see "that is, night golf at a corporate retreat."

So now that we've talked about what your retreat should *not* be, let's talk about an annual retreat for high-functioning teams or collections of direct reports who need to work like a team. What should happen? What should it feel like?

MY RETREAT RECIPE

Retreats take participants on a journey. At the most effective retreats, participants leave more engaged, more inspired, and reenergized about the mission and the road ahead. And this requires a great deal of work up front. I tell people you need six weeks' prep for the best offsite retreat. The ones who believe me see the payoff. Here are three things you need to include.

(1) Team Building/Ice Breaker

Stop! I saw you roll your eyes. If you believe as I do that it is important to manage in 3-D, then we need to offer opportunities for folks to share their full selves. Do not, I repeat, do not take this off the agenda because of moaning and groaning. The groaning comes from poor execution participants have experienced in the past.

But please don't let lousy ideas keep you from this critical piece of work at a retreat.

Here are two ideas that have never failed me.

The Foolproof Bio Book

I mean it. Foolproof. Folks will groan about homework and later they will thank you. A two-page bio. You can find a link to an example on my blog (http://www.joangarry.com/wp-content/uploads/2015/11/Joan-Garry-Personal-Bio1.pdf). Anything you want folks to know about you. Must include at least one picture and can't be a formal headshot. There must be some reference to why your organization is meaningful. No format off limits. Have had a CFO submit hers in Excel. A graphics person in cartoon form. Whatever works for a staff member and allows her to express who she is.

I like to start with a funny pop quiz to get the group warmed up at the start of the retreat. Then a discussion of the "ties that bind." Then a chance to ask colleagues questions about the bios. The range of issues that come up is stunning. I had one group in which the common thread was about nannies. A few had been raised by them. One woman resented the family her mom worked for as a nanny, and one board member had, in fact, been a nanny.

It was one of the most powerful (and riskiest) conversations I have had to navigate. It was about class and race and there were strong feelings in the room. With the generous spirit of the participants and a strong facilitative hand, it was a conversation that brought a diverse room together in the most remarkable way.

Bring a Thing

Ask every participant to bring *something* that reminds them why they are committed to the work of the organization. Give each person two minutes to describe the item and its significance. After everyone is done, place all items in a central location so they can be appreciated throughout the retreat. I will never forget a social justice attorney who brought a pretty, solid clay sculpture of what appeared to be a man behind a desk. The lawyer said (yes, with tears) that her son had made this for her. It was Attticus Finch from *To Kill A Mockingbird*. He wanted her to know that this is how he thought of her. (I can't even type that without tearing up.)

(2) Share the Vision

Board meetings and staff meetings are too tactical to be inspirational. Bring the work to life with a picture of the road ahead. In spite of challenges, it should be a journey no one wants to miss. I'm working with a head of school who is planning an offsite with her "team" because, based on meetings and conversations, there is not a shared vision of the education the school provides. In our next session, we will talk about language. Until you reach a shared sense of vision, you are a group and not a team.

> Bring the work to life with a picture of the road ahead.
> Until you reach a shared sense of vision, you are a group and not a team.

(3) Bring the Work to Life

I worked with a board a few years back for an organization that delivered produce to food pantries and shelters. It was so cold I wore gloves on my gloves. But I wanted to be able to lead the group with authenticity. At the board meeting, I was in the minority of folks who had touched the impact of the work by riding the truck to deliver that food.

If you are very clever, you can combine (1) and (3). Here's a great example. One organization I worked with offered a Friday night dinner to the clients—it had been going on for years. At the opening of the retreat, rather than a fancy social dinner, board members were asked to come to the dining hall. Their job: Talk to one client over dinner. They were asked to capture the client story. We began Saturday morning going around the room. Each person introduced themselves to the group as the client they had met the night before. Eighteen board members and 18 different characters, each touched by the organization in different ways. Then we put the names of each client on large Post-its on the wall. We'd reference them all through the day. What would Maria think about that long-term goal for the organization? Would it help *her?* It was crazy powerful.

A Few Words from the Leader

Here I want the leader to articulate her leadership style, to set out the charge for the group so that it can evolve into a team. *What do I need from this group of senior staff?* Is it simply a vehicle for sharing information or is the leader looking for creativity, dissent, pushback?

Assess How the Group Works

You have gotten some dimension from folks, the E.D. has shared the road ahead, and the work has come to life in a way that inspires you. Goose bump stuff. Now the question is posed: Are we, as the direct reports to the E.D. or as board members, working together as best as we possibly can to serve those clients? Are we a team or are we really a group? Do we appreciate what each of us brings to the table? Am I coming to these meetings to advocate for the interests of my own area or am I thinking of what's in the best interest of the clients, the community, the shelters, the food pantries? What's working? What could be working better? What do we need from one another to make this a stronger group—to maybe actually *deserve* to be called a team? What would need to change to get there?

A Time to Exhale

Do whatever you can to find a spot that enables the group to take a walk, get fresh air. If you can't, please just do not overschedule the day so that it feels breathless.

Appreciation

Every participant should feel valued for every dimension they bring to the work. I'm a big fan of a leader bestowing something unique and meaningful on each person there. It works well at the end. The simplest recommendation I make involves flowers. The leader bestows an individual flower on each person and when doing so, says something about the person that she or he appreciates. Each flower is different. At the end of that, there is a vase in the center of the room. All flowers get placed in the vase. The whole is greater than the sum of its parts.

Clear Actions and Follow-Up

Retreats are measured by what happens after them. Can a group volunteer to make sure that the action items really happen?

> Retreats are measured by what happens after them.

So what is all this in the service of? Ensuring the expectation that the collection of individuals must move in the direction of team behavior? Yup. Having a shared vision of where the organization is headed? Check.

One more important outcome of this kind of attention: retention.

KEEPING THE KEEPERS ON THE BUS

I had the privilege of interviewing Caroline Samponaro in a recent podcast (joangarry.com/samponaro). She has been with the same organization, Transportation Alternatives, for a decade. It feels almost unheard of in a land in which if I had a dime for every time I heard the word *burnout* . . .

Caroline was not burned out; not even close. And she could be. Every day she works with families who have experienced unimaginable loss. But nope, Caroline loves her job. She loves the people she works with, and she feels a deep sense of purpose. Her role in the organization has evolved over time, so she feels she is given regular opportunities to take on new challenges.

Daniel Pink has it right. It all starts with *purpose*. Harvard Business School and The Energy Project (a company that assesses workplace productivity) joined forces on a study. They found that the single most important influencer in job satisfaction and retention is purpose: *"Employees who derive meaning and significance from their work were more than three times as likely to stay with their organizations—the highest single impact of any variable."*

> The single most important influencer in job satisfaction and retention is purpose.

And why have I dedicated an entire chapter to what it takes to be a good manager in the nonprofit sector? Because really good managers build and retain great people. A great manager gives her staff member a clear picture of success, a voice, new opportunities, and appreciates the hell out of them. Financially when possible, and creatively when not.

There is one more "managerial" relationship we need to talk about. It's the trickiest of them all. The board and the executive director.

SUPERVISING AND EVALUATING THE EXECUTIVE DIRECTOR

I know. I know. I said it was a partnership. And yet the staff leader is accountable to the board. One of the board's core responsibilities is to hire and evaluate the executive director. Now I'm not taking back anything I said. I see a highly effective nonprofit as a twin-engine jet—two excellent engines that work in tandem. And yet, the ultimate buck stops with the board. If something bad happens (stay tuned for the next chapter!), you can fire the staff leader but it is the board that is ultimately responsible.

What makes this really tricky is that it's odd to have a boss who is a volunteer. And a volunteer who is, by design, only your boss for a finite portion of your entire tenure. And your boss isn't in the office next door. Actually, your boss might be halfway across the country and have another full-time job.

> What makes this really tricky is that it's odd to have a boss who is a volunteer.

I have found that there are a few things you must do to set this tricky relationship up to succeed. They tie back to everything we've been talking about throughout this chapter:

- *Regular meetings.* Not "we talk all the time" meetings. Biweekly with an agenda set out ahead and approved by both parties.
- *Annual goals.* Both parties *must* have a clear picture of success.
- *An annual evaluation.* It must be completed on or before the executive director's anniversary date. The top-line information must be shared with the full board. It cannot be done simply by the board chair, and I recommend engaging in some kind of 360-degree evaluation in which the executive director is evaluated by supervisors, colleagues, and staff. They are very helpful and, given that the board has only a single perspective, I argue that the information is more than just helpful—it's critical.
- *A contract or a detailed letter of employment.* This is absolutely necessary for retention, for succession planning, for risk management on the part of the organization should the relationship terminate, for smooth transitions, and for just good, old-fashioned clarity.

Your executive director deserves to be treated professionally and the preceding steps enable you to do that. Anything short of that is not only unprofessional, but risky.

If only organizations followed these clear and simple steps. If only executive directors were not defensive because they have a bias against volunteer bosses who don't really know what they do or really appreciate how hard they work. If only board chairs remembered that this process—of managing the executive director—is the most important and best opportunity to build that partnership I talk about—to offer good, solid feedback, to set clear goals, to appreciate the hell out of the passion and commitment and to the mission of the organization. And when it comes to compensation, to be thoughtful, generous when applicable, and creative about how to ensure that a five-star executive director is incented to stay.

Take it from me. I have heard every story at least twice. There was the executive director who was fired by the board while he was on vacation. I have worked with executive director clients who have been in their jobs for years and *never* had a performance review. I've seen them done so late it was as if the board was getting an early jump on the review for the following year. I've heard a board member say that he didn't write exactly what he thought about the executive director's performance because he was sure the executive director would figure out it was his comment. I have seen executive directors spending hours trying to figure out who said what. I have heard blow-by-blow defenses against every piece of constructive feedback. I have seen boards create evaluation instruments with absolutely no input (not talking decision here) from the executive director. I have heard a board try to include a noncompete clause. Yes, you heard that right. If you leave our organization in which you are an expert in the field of autism, you can't work for another autism organization for 12 months.

I am not making any of this up.

I just spent a chapter offering my insights on managing the paid and the unpaid. Please know that the best-managed organizations are well run from the top.

TWO THINGS EVERYONE IN YOUR ORGANIZATION WANTS

There really are only two things that anyone in your organization needs to be productive, to be a good team player, to manage generously, to give it their all.

• People in your organization want very badly to be successful.

> People in your organization want to be treated fairly and with compassion. It's not a lot to ask.

- People in your organization want to be treated fairly and with compassion.

Every single idea, suggestion, and insight included in this chapter will be no-brainers if viewed through the lens of these very simple needs.

"Ok, remember. You are the leader. You're going to need to pull yourself together."

Chapter 7   When It Hits the Fan

This is one of those book chapters you might feel compelled to skip. I, on the other hand, wouldn't consider writing a book on nonprofit leadership without addressing it head on because I hear comments like these all the time. *"I have enough challenges of the small and medium variety that I have trouble enough managing"* or *"If we focus on what we do well, we can avoid the big bad crises."*

This is also not a topic readers raise with me; thus you will not see a *Dear Joan* included in this chapter. No one ever asks me how to manage a crisis before it happens. But I am *regularly besieged* with emails about big, hot messes and how an organization can dig out. And, as I read them, I know they are often making things worse because they didn't have a plan.

You see, nonprofit leaders are by disposition an optimistic lot. They believe that with time, energy, smarts, strategy, and sheer will, they can improve society in ways large and small through their organization. It's one of the things I love about the people I

> Nonprofit leaders are by disposition an optimistic lot. So considering worse case scenarios is not exactly in their comfort zones.

work with. So fierce. So determined. So clear that if not them, then who? If not now, then when? I spend my days with folks like this and this attitude leads me to work harder for them.

So advocating that they take time to think about the worst possible thing that could happen to their organization, their sector, to a client? This kind of request can really fall on deaf ears. These fiercely determined, optimistic change agents don't want to go there.

But go there you must. Two reasons: First, leaders are expected to take the reins in times of crises. The great leader gives her community a sense of comfort that it will be handled well, that folks will be cared for, and that folks are working together. Now, the second reason: Leaders are wrong when they say that if they focus on doing good work, they can avert crises. It would be so lovely if this were true but it simply isn't.

In October 2013, a severely autistic 14-year-old boy named Avonte Oquendo walked out of his school in Queens, New York. He was in special education classes there and somehow eluded adult supervision and ran out of the building. His mom had told the school: "He likes to run." They were unprepared for what followed. There was such confusion, they believed that Avonte was in the building and a lockdown was ordered. More than an hour passed before they realized that Avonte was on the streets of New York City. The New York City Police Department pulled out all the stops to hunt for young Avonte. His parents grieved, hired a lawyer, and sued the city and the school.

Nearly a year later, his remains were found in the East River. So terribly tragic.

In June 2014, Greenpeace International lost $5.2 million based on a poorly timed, reckless investment. According to Greenpeace, the CFO acted beyond his authority and was terminated. *Five million dollars!* Based on how the story played out in the media, it was clear that a crisis management plan was not in place. Do we really think that announcing the termination of the CFO qualified as a crisis management plan? Might it have been smart and transparent for the treasurer of the board of Greenpeace International to come forward and take responsibility for being asleep at the switch? And that would be one of many decisions, messages, and actions Greenpeace should have been prepared to take.

On November 18, 1999, 12 students at Texas A&M University were killed and 26 others injured when the bonfire students were building in advance of their annual contest with rival University of Texas collapsed. This bonfire was an annual tradition for 100 years. Had Texas A&M taken precautions? Had it ever considered it was simply too dangerous to continue the tradition? And how did the university handle the tragedy and its aftermath? Yes, yes, and very well. More on that in a bit.

What about the sex abuse crisis at Penn State in 2012? The crisis and the public relations nightmare associated with assistant football coach Jerry Sandusky's criminal behavior became a story of international proportion. In deconstructing how the university handled the crisis, it's difficult to find a single thing the institution did right.

Lastly, Orlando, June 2016: The LGBT community and the world were rocked by the largest mass shooting in U.S. history at a gay bar. A shooting by a man claiming allegiance to an Islamic terrorist organization and, at the same time, clearly struggling with his own sexual identity. Hate crimes are not new to the LGBT community. It would hardly be a surprise to anyone that LGBT people are targets. Were the organizations advocating for LGBT equality ready for a crisis of this magnitude? Had there ever been strategy sessions with movement leaders to discuss how organizations might work together to spring into action on all fronts should a hate crime occur? I can speak from my own experience and say that, while I was at the helm of a gay rights organization, we had no plan, nor was there a movement strategy. I do not say that with pride. It's just a fact.

These are just a few examples. A report by the Institute for Crisis Management reports over 200,000 crisis stories in the news in 2016. While this number includes both corporate and public sector organizations, it is so important for nonprofit leaders to understand that if you haven't had a crisis yet in your nonprofit, it's probably not that you are good. It's more likely that you are lucky.

> If you haven't had a crisis yet in your nonprofit, it's probably not that you are good. It's more likely that you are lucky.

It could be argued that the nonprofit sector is in fact disproportionately affected by crisis. Why?

Nonprofits are often in the business of advocating for issues that are controversial—nay, *polarizing*. Oh, I don't know—say, gun control, for example. Debates can get ugly and go in very difficult directions.

If you are working for a marginalized community, you know full well that you have been climbing uphill for a long time. When communities like this get really tired, they can get vocal, they can impede your ability to move your organization forward, and if they feel your organization isn't doing absolutely everything to fix things, the anger can turn on you.

You may make a decision that your stakeholders disagree with—to close a program, to accept corporate sponsorship dollars from a company your stakeholder feels works against you.

You simply can't control for all things. A student suicide at a college or a university can happen suddenly. It can wreak havoc on the entire university community and present a real quandary for the institution about how to handle it with respect for the family and maintain the integrity of the institution.

Finally, let's talk about money. Manage it well and ensure that your revenue streams are diverse enough to sustain a precipitous drop in one category. A corporate sponsor with a change in leadership can lead to layoffs. Layoffs, reductions in services—these are crises. And you can build and steward relationships with the best of them but you are not the decision maker. And all the good work in the world may not change that funder's mind.

The issue may be internal. Like the Penn State scandal, there may be something profoundly wrong inside the organization. It could be the E.D., a board member, or a beloved staff member.

HOW ARE WE DEFINING *CRISIS*?

We need to have a common understanding of what we mean when we use the word. How do we distinguish from the crisis that falls under the category of "boy/girl who cried wolf?" Every one of us has encountered staff and board members who are what I like to call "fire alarm pullers." They get frantic before even counting to 10 to determine if what they have is a crisis.

My mother was a world-class fire alarm puller like this. I loved her dearly but her anxiety often led her to push her internal panic button. There was the time she thought her pacemaker alarm was going off and she promptly called 911. (As a known fire-alarm puller, my mother probably had one of the few telephone numbers they likely knew by heart.) Besides, you don't mess around with 89-year-olds. Emergency responders arrived on the scene within minutes only to find that her smoke alarm battery needed to be changed. My mom had assumed and created a crisis where one did not exist. And if you liked that anecdote, trust me when I say there are more where that one came from. So how do you know? Well, sometimes it couldn't be clearer. Sadly. You learn that an autistic kid at your school is missing. Clear, simple, and heart wrenching—a crisis, without a doubt. You learn that a finance staff member is embezzling money and the proof is in a report on your desk. That's another kind of crisis. You terminate an employee and maybe you have crossed at your T's and dotted all your I's and you wake up to a prominent piece in the local paper besmirching you and your organization. A crisis for sure.

According to Kathleen Fearn-Banks, author of *Crisis Communications: A Casebook Approach,* a crisis must have one or more of the following four key elements.

1. The incident damages the reputation and public opinion of the management or the organization.
2. The incident is so all-consuming that it interferes with the ability to get normal business done.
3. The incident leads to government or media scrutiny.
4. The situation leads to substantive loss of funding.

WHEN THE LIGHT AT THE END OF THE TUNNEL IS AN ONCOMING TRAIN

So here is the conversation that your standard do-gooder can't bear to have. And not only do they need to have it, but the board should hold the staff accountable to present a crisis management plan that is updated annually based on new information and context. It's time to pull a group of people together and start a real conversation to build a crisis management plan. This conversation, and the plan that evolves from it, could save your organization's reputation and the sustainability of your work, and it can, literally, save lives. Reread that last sentence if you had been previously unconvinced.

And if you are still unconvinced:

- Ask anyone who has been in the eye of the storm the degree to which they were consumed by the crisis.
- Ask anyone who has been in the eye of the storm how demoralizing it was.
- Ask anyone who has been in the eye of the storm how little time the storm left them to the do the other 99 percent of their jobs.

As you consider what I call the "oncoming trains," you cannot be timid. You have to say the things no one really wants to say out loud. As a leader, you must be a model for your staff and the rest of the board. You must create an environment in which staff and board feel empowered enough to share bad news and potentially bad news. You must be sure they understand that it is their job to speak up and that this is a sign of strength, not weakness.

Two-thirds of all crises should never make it to the level of "crisis." From the top of the management chain to the bottom of the organization food chain, everyone should always be on the lookout for those little problems or issues that, ignored or underestimated, can grow into a full-blown public nightmare.

—*Larry Smith, Senior Consultant, Institute for Crisis Management*

BUILDING A CRISIS MANAGEMENT PLAN

Please do not be daunted by all of this. This plan, incorporating some of the wisdom of Kathy Bonk and Emily Tynes from their book, *Strategic Communications for Nonprofits,* can be developed in less than a day by a core group of folks. It would be great to include the board chair. She or he will be in the hot seat and it will create ownership and buy-in.

Only a day, you say? Or less? Yes. Because the real truth is that if you peek under your pillow, there is a small bag of worry dolls, each of them representing the things that keep you up at night. The really big things will serve as the list for Phase I.

Phase I: What's the Worst Thing that Could Happen?

Begin by developing a list that includes situations I would consider blazes of the five-alarm variety. I really don't like having to type these.

- A child in your charge is missing.
- A teacher has been accused of abusing a student.
- A hate crime is committed against the community you represent.
- A shooting takes place in the office of your organization.
- A college student commits suicide.
- A change in your programs will enrage your clients.
- Eighty-five percent of your revenue comes from a single source that decides to pull funding.
- Your staff or board leader is charged with a crime.
- A credible report is issued that is widely reported. It makes a strong case for misuse of funds.
- A staff termination leads to a lawsuit, resulting in staff unrest, negative publicity, and key funders walking away.

Have you broken out in a cold sweat yet? Okay, hang on. I'll get you there with this next exercise.

Phase II: What's the Worst Headline You Could See About Your Organization on the Front Page of *The New York Times?*

You may think this is the same exercise, but please stay with me. We'll come back to headlines a bit further along in the chapter. Right now, I want you to create these as a benchmark. And as you do this, I also think you should visualize the photo that will accompany the headline. The photos often stay with folks much longer than the words.

One last word of advice here: Don't get *too* carried away. Just pick three or four scenarios and flesh them out. Make sure that one is about an internal decision the organization makes and then three others that are potential crises. You don't need a long list, as the plans will have common threads.

Phase III: What Assumptions Will Be Made?

Here you are trying, in each of your nightmarish scenarios, putting yourself in the shoes of the press, the board, the public, the staff, and donors. What will they think and feel when they find out? I'll give you a big, fat hint here. People will always assume that you didn't do enough right away. And what kind of actions can you take or messages can you deliver (and how quickly) to get out in front before assumptions are made? Make a list of assumptions for each scenario and then actions or messages that may preempt those assumptions.

Phase IV: Outline a Process

The process should have several important elements:

1. *An Organization Crisis Management Team.* It clearly needs to include the E.D. and the board chair. But there will be lots to do because "it" will be flying. Here's what you need:
   - A point person for the media. Typically, the leader. Should the leader be at the heart of the crisis—legal or criminal—a backup should be identified.
   - If you have a communications staffer, they clearly get pegged.
   - It can be *very* helpful to have someone who is not part of the day-to-day work—a volunteer or donor you ask to be a part of this in the event of a 911 situation. Perhaps someone who works at a PR agency in your community? Having an outside perspective can help you avoid a bunker mentality—feeling like this is all you talk and think about and believing that the entire universe is talking and thinking about it.
   - Someone who will monitor the media (this could be a volunteer role), set Google alerts, and stay on top of the buzz and how it is playing out. Things move quickly and the team needs to have its finger on the pulse.

2. *The "Antidote" Headline You Most Want to See in the Paper.* Time to compare and contrast the "worst" one from Phase I. Create the headline for each of your two to four crisis scenarios and then back into core messages from the headlines.

3. *Training Spokespeople for the World of 911.* Is there any way that anyone in your community can, after the development of the plan, offer the crisis management two- to three-hour training pro bono? Or what about the communications person at another, larger organization in town who has been

through this training? This is a specialized kind of training—high-stress and high-intensity.

4. *Build Ally Relationships Before You Need Them Badly.* When you have developed relationships with elected officials, business leaders, and other nonprofit leaders in your community, your organization is richer for it. You are more informed about the goings on, you have the opportunity to be of help to one another, and, in a crisis situation, you will be there for them and *they will be there for you.* You will need external validators who know about your good work and your integrity—who can publicly support you and privately offer you guidance. This may be the last item on the list but don't think for one second it is the least important. It takes a village to manage through a crisis.

SO NOW YOU ARE ALL SET FOR WHEN IT HITS THE FAN, RIGHT?

Time for three little secrets:

1. *Even with a plan, you are never really ready.* You are prepared but not really ready. When you are in the eye of the storm, there is an ingredient that blurs, causes short-term memory loss of all this planning. It's called emotion. It manifests itself in everything from self-doubt to defensiveness to panic. And that, my friends, is why planning is so important. Because you have a road map you can focus on and know that you have done your best to be prepared.

True story: A direct service organization has to move out of its current space. The new space identified has many plusses that will enable the organization to offer better services but is outside the core neighborhood of the community it serves. That neighborhood is now prohibitively expensive. Clients are in an uproar and, more importantly, the figurehead founder has gone to the press to condemn the decision. The quote is also mean-spirited toward the current E.D. and board. This founder is a big personality in the community and in the organization's 20-plus-year history. He has been a go-to person for the press—often more than the current organizational leadership.

Not to sound like a shrink, but how do you think that E.D. feels? Hurt? Angry that he was not sought out? Defensive about the decision? Upset that the clients are upset because these are the folks whose lives you are there to improve. Now *that* is a lot of emotion. Having a plan helps keep that in check.

2. *Nonprofit leaders tend to be pleasers who look for middle ground.* (Is that a common theme in this book? I'm thinking yes.) That is frequently *not* the answer to a crisis. More often that not, crisis management is about bold leadership, clear decision making, and sticking to your guns on what might be unpopular decisions.

I'm remembering a situation a community center found itself in. The center was in a major urban setting and one of its offerings was space rental for meetings. An Israeli organization reserved space, much to the chagrin of a Palestinian organization. The organization focused on trying to make both sides happy and met with each group often. Not a bad strategy, but solving the Israeli-Palestinian conflict was well above this leader's pay grade.

The issue wasn't about solving the conflict. The issue was developing a clear policy about who could and who could not rent space in the center. Did all organizations interested in renting space need to share the core values of the community served by the center? And don't think for a minute that every member of the community was like-minded. There needed to be an assessment of the rental policy. The organization's leadership—board and staff—needed to own and buy in to any changes. It needed to be presented, a stake placed in the ground, and all live with the consequences. The bottom line:

Someone is likely to be very unhappy. Leadership is not about making people happy— it's about making decisions that are in clear alignment with the mission and values of your organization. And a lack of clarity can ignite a crisis. Or make matters worse.

> Leadership is not about making people happy— it's about making decisions that are in clear alignment with the mission and values of your organization. And a lack of clarity can ignite a crisis.

3. In a crisis, you won't want to make the wrong decision and being deliberate could result in moving too slowly. You will want all the facts before you move. You won't have them. Trust me. But those who learn about the crisis want information faster, way faster than you are comfortable providing it. And if you don't provide it, someone other than you will fill the void— inaccurately or not in your favor.

Figure out what you can say ASAP that (1) is totally authentic, (2) honors the need for information, (3) makes a commitment to frequent communications and continued updates, and (4) reiterates the integrity of your organization as a core value and your commitment to doing what it takes to be true to that throughout the crisis and its resolution.

For example: The massacre in Orlando at the gay nightclub broke to the press sometime around 6 A.M. on Sunday, June 12, 2016. It was known by 6:30 A.M. that it was a gay nightclub. We didn't know how many were dead—at that time they were saying 20. Nor did we know how many of the injured or deceased would be gay. That said, LGBT community leaders know the significance of gay nightclubs as places of freedom, safety, and celebration.

It was only at roughly noon that any LGBT organization had added this story to the home page of its website. I went to

CNN, *The New York Times Digital Edition*, and to every gay organization website. Nothing. We all knew enough by 7 A.M. to put a banner on the homepage and a link to a major news story. Or a statement (or eblast) by 8 A.M. that said simply, "We don't know much but we do know *this*. Our community has been targeted in what looks to be one of the worst mass shootings in U.S. history. Our hearts are broken for everyone in that club and their families. Here's a link to what we *do* know. And you can count on us at XYZ organization to be doing A, B, and C in the hours and days to come. Our family at XYZ grieves with all of you." Maybe a simple image. A rainbow flag at half-mast?

Yes, it was a Sunday at 6:30 A.M. But shouldn't organizations that fight for the marginalized, who are often the victims of hate crimes, have a crisis management strategy and rapid response capability? This is what makes a nonprofit great.

IS A CRISIS PREVENTABLE?

Don't you just hate it when a good question gets asked and the answer is, "It depends"? But it does depend on the nature of the crisis. That said, there are often clues.

Could the LGBT community have prevented the attack at the Pulse nightclub? No. Were there clues that Omar Mateen had a plan? Yes. When a student takes his or her own life on a college campus, were there missed clues that the student was deeply troubled? Yes. The assistant head football coach at Penn State was accused of sexual abuse—were there clues? Yes. At Texas A&M, had there ever been injuries to students while building a massive bonfire? Yes. If a staff member were embezzling, wouldn't there be some oddity in the financial statement? Yes.

But do we see the clues? And if we do, as I mentioned earlier, is the culture of the organization such that there is a receptivity to sharing those clues and is there a proactive culture that leads to exploration of those clues?

Crisis management expert Kathleen Fearn-Banks talks about the four phases of an organizational crisis:

1. The prodromal phase (aka "Look closely and you'll see it coming")
2. The acute phase (aka "eye of the storm")
3. The chronic phase (aka "Please let this stop!")
4. Resolution (aka "There were actually a few minutes today when I didn't think about this")

The "clues" I noted earlier occur are what Fearn-Banks calls "prodromes."

Prodromes are often right there. Clear for the right people to see. I remember thinking during the Penn State crisis: *"With a crisis of this magnitude,* someone *had to know."* And, of course, someone did know.

Eleven years before the scandal became public, the *president* of Penn State was alerted by two key staff members: the VP of administration and campus police and the athletic director. These staffers reported that assistant football coach Jerry Sandusky had been seen in the showers "horsing around" with a naked minor boy. The president of Penn State asked two simple questions: "Are you sure that was how it was described—'horsing around?'" The second question he asked the men: "Are you sure that was all that was reported?" He received affirmative responses to both of his questions. And nothing was done . . . for *11 years.*

WHAT CRISIS MANAGEMENT SHOULD LOOK LIKE

Penn State made too many mistakes to count. And frankly, it is easier to find examples of missteps than it is to find strong leadership in crisis.

So a few minutes deconstructing the Texas A&M bonfire crisis is instructive. Led by the executive director of university relations, the university was on its A-game from start to finish.

Only five months into her job at the time of the tragedy, Cynthia Lawson was not a stranger to crisis—but in the private sector. Fifteen years earlier, she was an executive at a large utility company building a nuclear power plant. You bet they had a crisis plan and they even practiced it annually. She had no idea how ideal that experience was for what she encountered at Texas A&M.

During her first five months, she invested a good deal of time developing relationships with folks inside and outside the university—from media to elected officials to business owners to colleagues at other institutions of higher education.

As I mentioned earlier, in the 100-year history of the bonfire, there had been no casualties as a result of the collapse of the bonfire. There were rigorous instructions and close attention was paid by students to ensure that the utmost care was taken. So in her first five months, Lawson was not aware of any prodromes or clues.

The moment of the collapse began the acute phase of the crisis. It was the middle of the night. Lawson was the point person and shouldered a good deal of the work until the morning. She held four or five news conferences the first *day,* ensuring that the media had what it needed in the most efficient way. She also used journalists (the ones she had built relationships with) to get the word out about what was needed—food, cell phones, batteries, blankets. The media became a mouthpiece to promote a hotline parents could call. It became a community effort and not a blame game. There were key messages and everyone stuck to them, including students who wanted to be of help. One of them was, of course, care and concern for injured and deceased students and their parents. Another one included facts about the bonfire tradition that put what seemed to be an irresponsible activity into context. Lastly, there was a message about how special the Texas A&M community was and that, together, the community would get through this and be there to support one another.

The hotline and the website they set up especially for this fed the media everything they needed. The university's internal communications fed information to student government, residence hall staff, university trustees, and other stakeholder groups so no one felt left out of the loop. Everyone had the key messages ingrained, and everyone had specific ways in which they could help. The entire process was proactive and transparent.

The chronic phase of this crisis—when the story was still front-page news lasted two weeks with plenty of coverage continuing for months. During this time, an outside person was appointed to lead a commission to investigate the incident. Again, Lawson was supportive and proactive.

Also during this time, negative stories emerged and Lawson's approach was simple and clear: The university would make no comments that could interfere with the investigative commission's work.

The resolution phase began with the report from the commission. The commission found that a safe bonfire would have been possible had the school taken the right measures before and during its construction. There were lawsuits and the bonfire tradition was moved off campus and, ultimately, discontinued.

Even though she got through this crisis in stellar fashion without a plan, she likely was poised and prepared because of her prior experience in the private sector.

THE MOST COMMON NONPROFIT CRISIS: FINANCIAL CRISIS AND LAYOFFS

I am often called upon to help a nonprofit executive director pull an organization out of a fiscal crisis, so I'd be remiss to write a chapter called "When It Hits the Fan" without talking about the most common, and often the most chronic, crisis nonprofits face.

What can it look like? There are several common scenarios—each of them, frankly, way too common.

A brand new E.D. arrives on the scene and learns that the organization is in the depths of a fiscal crisis. Did the board mention this during the interview process? Yes. Maybe they even showed you some numbers. But it isn't until you open those books and sit down with the staff member responsible for keeping them that the reality of it hits.

Why didn't the board tell you the truth? They might have told you the truth as they knew it. As it was told to them by the predecessor. They might not have known. Please do not get me started on board members who shirk their responsibility to understand the basic finances of the organization. It is not *solely* the job of the treasurer. And, sometimes, to be honest, the treasurer is asleep at the switch, too. Then, of course, we have pleaser executive directors fearful of sharing bad news. There is a whole lot of intersecting dysfunction at play in this kind of scenario.

Another is what I call the accident waiting to happen. The organization's revenue diversity isn't diverse. Most of its eggs are in a single basket—one big donor, one significant special event, one very large government grant or, most often, the annual gala. Something goes awry. The big donor has a fallout with a senior member of your organization or decides the organization is too dependent on you (duh) and decides to take a year or so off. New leadership at the donor corporation means new priorities, or a request for impact metrics you can't deliver on time. The gala is canceled because it is scheduled on the heels of the 2008 market crash. Or there is a snowstorm— the honoree is a no-show and the silent auction tanks because folks are not in the house.

One or more of these happen and—*poof*—you are sweating payroll. You are making decisions about which vendors to pay and whose calls should go to voicemail. Paid staff is anxious, wants assurances, and knows they are not forthcoming. You meet with your board chair. She wants an expense reduction plan. You want a board that is going to step up and fill the gap.

How do you manage *this* kind of crisis? You follow the same basic recipe. You are authentic, transparent, and proactive. I have worked with clients with whom we used the crisis as an opportunity to teach everyone Nonprofit Finance 101. We used a very simple dashboard that could be easily explained to *everyone* around the table. Download the PDF at joangarry .com/financial-dashboard. What works about this is that it is not a page filled with numbers. It is a page filled with *the most important* numbers. The other helpful thing is that the numbers are put in the context of the *healthy* numbers you want. This just drives me crazy about finance presentations—*no frame of reference!* It would be like going to the doctor and getting a report that your LDL cholesterol is 215. And that is *all* they tell you. *Board and staff need to know what the numbers mean and what they* ought to be!

Speaking of high cholesterol and personal health, I used a personal medical metaphor when keeping staff apprised of our financial situation. At my first meeting, GLAAD was on a fiscal respirator. We moved to breathing on our own, then to a step-down unit, and so on. It brought the challenges to life for folks and they felt very much a part of what was happening. And just like a doctor, I answered the questions I could and was honest about what I couldn't. *"Will there be layoffs?"* In that first week, I was clear and adamant that I was working with the board and doing everything in my power to avoid them *but* I could make no promises. As we moved from dire straits, I was still unable to make promises but they could see the improved health for themselves and understand that things were getting better.

In financial crisis situations, I wish more organizations would focus on driving revenue rather than expense reductions. I am working with one client whose biggest source of revenue was a single corporate sponsor who dropped out. This client identified some foundation money for capacity building to bring us in to identify other corporate sponsors and to build an individual giving program. The organization is now steady with a diverse revenue portfolio.

> In financial crisis situations I wish more organizations would focus on driving revenue rather than expense reductions.

And, as for the rapid-fire fundraising that you may need to do, be aggressive without being desperate. Be honest and own the fact that, based on how the organization evolved, your revenue streams were not diverse enough. You saw this coming (a clue, or prodrome) and you were unable to be nimble enough to build capacity in the other revenue lines. You can make this work.

I was fundraising for payroll early in my tenure and I was right in the eye of the cash flow storm. A donor suggested a very expensive restaurant. I'll admit it. I was sweating. Dinner was lovely and the donor was engaged. I was new and shared my vision and she got it. I talked around the money challenges but I must have made the need clear. I asked for $25,000 and she said, "Yes." But she went one step further. *"I'm hearing a bit of urgency here—would it be helpful if my business manager wired the funds tomorrow?"* My development director and I nearly wept. We said yes as calmly as we could. And, yes, the donor took care of dinner. We knew we could meet payroll. That was the first time I ever did a jig in a parking garage.

If your senior-level conversation turns to expense reductions and possible layoffs, many of the lessons of this chapter will be of value. The choices you make must be smart and strategic. If money really is a challenge, take the time to examine your programs. Is there anything that is not mission-critical? This can be described as working on "mission focus" and position the expense reductions as strategic. Is there a way to offset that a message about program elimination or cost reductions with a board chair message? Indicate that the board is making a renewed commitment to individual giving fundraising so that a new development officer can be hired to move the organization from its dependence on event revenue.

And if, after all this, your plan must include layoffs, I encourage you to read the communications plan outlined for the departure of the rock star staff leader in the next chapter. I beg you to be equally methodical about how the information is communicated and to whom and in what order.

And don't forget an important step. Layoffs are not just about those who have lost their jobs. In my experience, staff and board leaders neglect the folks still in the house. They are relieved and yet deeply saddened about their colleagues. Maybe they are angry because they disagree with the choices. They know that they are about to have more work added to an already overflowing plate. And, of course, the question *"Am I next?"* pulses through their veins.

Oh, and when you do sit with them, there is one phrase I ask you to avoid: *"Well I guess we are all going to have to do more with less."* If this is your mindset, don't sit with them until you have had an attitude adjustment. In many situations, staff is *always* under-resourced and it is a source of frustration, anger, and burnout. Please don't make it worse.

Then there is *external* messaging. All of it should reinforce the importance of your work. Never forget to focus on why the work of your organization matters. And please engage your board in the public comments. The board often sits on the sideline and leaves the staff leader to carry the water in these situations. Your organization is always perceived to be stronger when the public sees that strong partnership—in good times and in times when your organization is in the financial ICU.

THE MAIN THING

> The main thing is to keep the main thing the main thing.
>
> —*Stephen Covey*

The moral of this chapter rests in Covey's statement. At some point in your leadership, there will be a crisis. It will be one that comes out of nowhere or one that could have been nipped in the bud (more likely the latter). How you handle it will be a key component of your identity as a leader.

Before I spell out the moral, compare and contrast the crises at Texas A&M and the one at Penn State. What was the "main thing" at each institution?

I would argue that the main thing at Penn State was to protect the reputation of the institution at all costs, even if that meant a coverup of nearly heinous proportions. Penn State had a terminal case of institutional arrogance. At Texas A&M, the main thing was, first and foremost, to do whatever it took to take care of students and their parents. Texas A&M was a central element in a caring community and their objective throughout was simply to do the right thing.

So let's go back to talking about the moral to be gleaned from these anecdotes. You could say that the moral is "be ready for that crisis when it hits" and you would not be wrong. But that's not the only answer. I believe another answer is that you have to create a culture in which good news *and* difficult news are received well.

But what is the most important answer? Stephen Covey, the author of 7 *Habits of Highly Effective People* nails it. It's about understanding your organization's *main thing* and keeping that main thing the main thing throughout your leadership tenure.

Let's say you run a homeless shelter and a minor is abused by a staff member (I hate even writing that), the main thing is tied directly to your mission. You are about the care of kids who need homes and caring environments. *Be that* if something heinous happens. Communicate as quickly as possible with whatever you know. And go ahead and be clear that you will be outraged if you find out if there is truth to the accusation and that *you* will lead the charge to get to the bottom of it. If it's true, you will make the changes necessary—not just with that individual—but with recruitment, background checks, hiring, and evaluation. You are an advocate for these kids. Just because one person engaged in heinous activity does not diminish your passion and commitment to care for these kids. Keep that main thing the main thing.

Remember the direct service organization that relocated and the founder used the media as a bullhorn to mobilize clients to protest and wreaked havoc on the image of the organization in the media (and to some funders)?

First off, the behavior of the founder, through the years, offered plain clues that she would potentially make an effort to undermine the organization should it make a strategic move that she felt was the wrong one. She was a walking prodrome. With lots of media access.

Perhaps relationships were not cultivated and called upon—folks who could have been credible, external spokespeople about the opportunities the move presented. Was the founder brought in and honored early enough in the process? And what kind of communications plan was in place so that the clients understood what was happening when and what the dramatic improvements in service the new space would afford?

I don't know, but a strong answer to those questions would make a big difference. The organization did not control the messaging. The founder did. As a result, the acute phase lasted for a painfully long time.

Did the organization lose clients as the founder predicted? No. The organization was able to retain current clients and grow its base with added space and services. There were other accusations that did not come to pass. But, because the founder controlled the messaging, the crisis was prolonged and the organization's reputation took a hit.

I read recently that Cynthia Lawson has retired after a distinguished career in higher education and as a national expert on crisis management. So none of you can hire her to consult with you as you proactively build a plan of your own. Although that would be mighty nice.

Instead, you have the kick in the pants I just spent most of this chapter giving you. Please take it to heart. Invest a day. And start the day by agreeing on one thing as a group. *What is your organization's main thing?* Write it in a big font on a flip chart and keep it

> What is your organization's main thing?

front and center throughout your discussion about how you would handle crisis. It will be your North Star.

If you can build a plan that enables you to keep the main thing the main thing, you will be a leader that everyone who touches and is touched by the work will admire and respect.

That may not be the *main* thing but that is a good thing—a very good thing.

"At a two-hour executive session, they mentioned something about me getting hit by a bus. Is this about succession planning or should I be paranoid?"

Chapter 8   Hello, I Must Be Going
(Or, Navigating Leadership Transitions)

I hope I have been making a strong case for the joy and privilege of joining a nonprofit organization as a leader, either paid or unpaid. My conversion in 1997 at the age of 39 was personally and professionally transformative and I could not recommend nonprofit work highly enough. I'm nearly evangelical about it (thus, this book!).

I believe I have also made the case that these roles are not easy. They take a big toll on people. Folks in your organization are relying on you to *lead*—it's a lot of pressure and stress. And I'm sure there are days when you'd like nothing more than to just follow. I remember telling my wife once about a discussion I had with a gathering of a group of executive directors. She asked me what the discussion was about. I realized that, most of the time, folks talked about how difficult their jobs were and how they fantasized about resigning. She said wisely (as she so often does), *"These are capable people. Why don't they just go get jobs they don't have to complain about?"*

I gave that comment some thought. In conversations like these, I could typically identify those who just wanted to kvetch with the kindred spirits who would totally understand and empathize with the frustrations of the role.

And then there were the others. There was a tone that told me it was deeper than the kind of kvetching you do with kindred spirits. Clearly, we know passion is a key driver—maybe the fire in their belly about the organization was evolving into smoldering embers. Maybe they have made a few poor hires and those folks are trying their very last nerves. Maybe they just can't figure out how to get the board to do anything and have lost the oomph to do their part to fully engage their board. Maybe they have just been in the job too long, really need a change, and are allowing inertia to take hold.

These are the folks who respond to new, energetic voices with *"Oh, we tried that and it didn't work."* Or a suggestion to try something new with the board is met with *"Oh, they will never do that."* Then there is the leader who doesn't have the energy to let a staff member go when it is really necessary. Everyone on staff sees it. And the defense is: *"My development director isn't great but she's not the worst. And good development directors are hard to find."* If you are on a board and you hear this, this should be a big, fat, red flag. Your staff leader is beginning to *settle*. And when you are in the business of changing the world, the folks counting on you deserve way more than "not the worst."

This is a staff leader who probably needs to be asked to step off the bus. But what if there is no egregious performance problem (there often isn't—it's just mediocrity)? What is an organization to do?

Then there is the five-star staff leader who just knows when it is time to call it quits. Perhaps the E.D. realizes that a younger leader with new energy is what the organization needs. Maybe the E.D. has been offered a bigger and better job elsewhere. Or maybe the work is too intense and it's time to create a better work and life balance in a different kind of role. This kind of transition is easier for the organization in one sense—no tough decisions to make. But losing a five-star leader rocks an organization to its core. And this kind of transition transfers power to a board that may or may not be prepared or capable of handling it.

> Losing a five-star leader rocks an organization to its core.

And what about that board and *its* leadership? That's a different ballgame altogether.

Some board chairs are reluctant leaders. They have been what I like to call "volun*told*." Some of these leaders come without a really good sense of what the role entails. In many ways, they have actually signed up for a second full-time job and someone neglected to mention that. So often, while they likely come with a good amount of "belly fire," they often *feel* or actually *are* ill-equipped for the job. Many would step down in a heartbeat if someone offered to take their spot.

There's another kind of board leader who poses a different challenge. The rock star board chair. The one who throws everything she has into the role. Maybe she is retired or doesn't like her job and giving 120 percent to the role is just what *she* needs. Now how could that possibly be a problem? Two scenarios—neither great for the greater good.

SCENARIO NUMBER ONE

I have a client like this. Let's call her Mary. She is a real rock star—smart, strategic, and giving the board chair role all she's got. And she's got a *lot*. I remind her regularly, *"You have to make this job actually seem doable to someone else on the board."* This kind of rock star can actually weaken a board—no need to step up; Mary has it all covered. She or he does not see board-building as part of what makes her a rock star. And when this kind of rock star steps down, there is a void of strong leadership and there is a big risk that the board will become rudderless.

SCENARIO NUMBER TWO

Or what if Suzie the board chair gives 120 percent but *isn't* a rock star. Maybe she rules autocratically. Micromanages the staff, but the board isn't aware of challenges with the staff because Suzie does it all. She tells everyone what to do and they give it their best shot. The board reluctantly follows and knows things are not quite right but (a) doesn't know how to navigate a transition or (b) no one is willing to step in.

Let's add one more complication. What if there are no term limits for board service in your by-laws? Or more likely, you have them but don't enforce them. There isn't even any boundary to the length of service you can count on to shift leadership to someone else. Suzie could serve as chair for decades. The result? Weak board members are perfectly satisfied that someone else is in charge and strong board members head for the hills. And oh, by the way, without term limits (or the enforcement of them), you can forget about a recruitment process that builds a leadership pipeline.

> And oh, by the way, without term limits (or the enforcement of them), you can forget about a recruitment process that builds a leadership pipeline.

You're depressed now, right? Please don't be. Stay with me. I needed to outline the permutations and combinations of organizational leadership and the transitions the organization needs and the ones the organization is hoping won't happen anytime soon so we can start to tackle the "how." Each of these situations—with both paid and unpaid personnel—require different strategies and tactics.

But these strategies and tactics must be in the service of a larger goal that no one—and I mean *no one*—can forget. Leadership transitions are the most destabilizing forces in the life of a nonprofit. Every single choice you make and how you make it—whether you are stepping down or whether you are asking someone to step down—must be done with the utmost integrity, the highest possible transparency, and with a respect for the staff, volunteers, donors, and other key stakeholders who are in need of constant assurance that the organization is steady, focused, and with five-star person power and smart strategy, is driving at full speed in the pursuit of its mission.

SO ARE THESE FOLKS GOOD AT THEIR JOBS?

Before I offer you strategies for contending with the scenarios I outlined earlier, we have to answer a key question. And the question is as relevant on the board side as it is on the staff side: *How are these people doing at their jobs?* Here I am calling one a "rock star" and in another case, talking about asking one to step off the bus. And is the mediocre staff leader *really* mediocre? Says who? And based on what criteria?

I have now worked with hundreds of clients across many sectors with annual budgets from $500,000 to $70 million. Do

> Do you want to know how many E.D.s I encounter who receive formal, annual reviews from the board? I guess "hardly any" isn't really a number, is it?

you want to know how many E.D.s I encounter who receive formal, annual reviews from the board? I guess "hardly any" is not really a number, is it? But that is the correct answer. Really? Really. Why not? I wish I better understood the answer to this. It is one of three fundamental responsibilities of a nonprofit board: *Hire, evaluate, and fire (if necessary) the chief executive.*

Do boards not know? Hard to believe, right? Board members are typically employees who expect and receive annual performance reviews. Why would an E.D. be different? Are boards lazy? I don't think so. People who join boards are infrequently lazy people—in fact, they are usually high-performers and Type A personalities. Does it just fall off the to-do list? And does the E.D. not remind them because she or he thinks the board can't effectively evaluate because they are not engaged? I don't know the answers—I suppose each circumstance is different.

Here's what I do know: an annual performance review that evaluates the executive on the accomplishment of goals that have been approved by the board as part of the *last* annual review process is a nonnegotiable activity. And here's a concrete suggestion for ensuring that it gets done, gets done fairly, and gets done on time.

Recruit an HR professional to your board. Every board should have one. Give that person the responsibility to develop a process and to hold board leadership accountable to execute it. No one in sight for board recruitment? Ask someone to serve as your pro bono human resources consultant—a few hours a month for leadership evaluation and some consulting time on high-level staff hiring and firing decisions. In exchange, offer your pro bono HR consultant visibility for his company on the website or gala invites. People liked to be asked to volunteer to do very targeted things that are seen as valuable.

You can do this. You should do this. To be a professional, grown-up board, you need to do this. And it needs to be multidimensional (a 360)—I spoke about this in an earlier chapter. As board members, you do not and cannot have the full picture. And it is the only avenue staff may have to raise big concerns without fear of repercussions.

Your staff leader is not the *only* person whose performance needs to be evaluated. Your board chair needs an evaluation, too. (Stop laughing! I heard you. Keep reading!)

Unlike executive director evaluations that actually do happen, albeit infrequently, I cannot think of a single client who has conducted some kind of evaluation of the board leader. I know why. The board doesn't want to know the answer because (a) the board chair reluctantly agreed and we don't want to push him out; (b) there is no one else who would do it; (c) the person who could do it said, "No" each of the five times she was asked; or (d) it could mean that they ask *you!*

But it's a dirty little secret in the nonprofit space (now that it is in my book, maybe not quite so secret). Do you know how many executive directors either jump ship to another gig or burn out because the board chair is weak or unavailable or micromanaging or unethical? Me neither, but it is way more than you think and way more than most people know. Because E.D.s don't tell. Executive directors are not quick to raise serious concerns about their board chairs. First, while I refer to it as a partnership (and I believe that), the buck stops with the board chair. The E.D. sees that hierarchy—the board chair is my boss. Second, who will they tell?

> Executive directors are not quick to raise serious concerns about their board chairs.

Here's a hypothetical. The board chair takes the job as chair for the wrong reason. It's presented as altruistic and downright noble. But she raises her hand because she needs power in her life. Maybe her husband just left her. The board chair makes the life of the E.D. miserable and provides direction directly to staff that runs counter to the E.D.'s instructions. The E.D. writes emails late at night, maybe after a few cocktails. They are tough, sometimes bordering on offensive. The E.D. starts to feel like the chair wants him out. Maybe she wants the job for herself?

But it's hard to see that in the boardroom. As a fellow board member, maybe you feel some tension but are not totally sure what that is about. And then some other board issue comes up and it flies out of your head. The E.D. has no formal avenue to raise concerns—no one asks him. Another two years under her thumb? No, thank you. The E.D. jumps ship.

It happens *all the time*. I work with clients, strategizing about how to find allies on the board to talk to about concerns. It's not easy. I talk about building leadership capacity and a pipeline on the board so that everyone (board and E.D.) can see board members in action as chairs of committees and be evaluated by all to see if board leadership is right for them. But it takes time. And even the best committee chair can falter as a board chair.

Again, I point to HR support from outside. This means a facilitated conversation by the HR person (or even a certified mediator) to talk through what's working and what's not working. Perhaps a memo from that person to the governance committee of the board. Another route is the co-chair model. This can work nicely because it can be a thought partnership of three, offering differing perspectives. Second, if one chair is weak, the other sees it as well, so the E.D. has someone else in his corner. The strong co-chair and the E.D. can strategize or work around the more challenging co-chair.

There are no doubt other answers and strategies—perhaps you have come up with even better ones in your organization, but, to reiterate, boards must evaluate executive directors and the board must provide checks and balances on the performance of the board chair in her capacity as the supervisor of the executive.

This was not a digression from the topic at hand: Who stays and who goes? Without an evaluation process, how can a board possibly know? I have found that there are archetypes for board and staff leaders and each one presents unique challenges.

Let's look at each of these types of leaders. What work should these leaders do—internal soul searching, planning, or both? And how do the deciders manage a decision that has been made or engage in making one in a way that serves the mission of the organization well?

So let's assume we have a formal process for evaluation and thus a fair assessment of the paid and unpaid leadership of your organization. Let's look at each of these types of leaders. What work should these leaders do—internal soul searching, planning, or both? And how do the deciders manage a decision that has been made or engage in making one in a way that serves the mission of the organization well?

Lastly, let's call it out. The buck always stops with the board. The board, as a collective, is the final decider about what leadership in the organization needs to look like. The executive director (even a founder) does not have the final say. The board calls the shots when it comes to leadership. This one sentence alone should be incentive enough to make a commitment to recruiting and retaining the most excellent people and to building a most excellent board. So let's start with board leadership.

BOARD LEADERSHIP GONE AWRY

Here's what you are going for:

- A board that understands its role
- Individuals who are clear about what successful board service looks like

- Functioning committees with chairs who are exercising and demonstrating leadership
- A commitment to ongoing identification of board prospects and, thus, a strong list of prospective board members
- A path to board leadership (usually by way of committee leadership) that has given the prospective new leader a test drive and the board and the executive director are on the same page about the best choice
- A five-star board chair who leads and manages the board and partners with the E.D. so they can lead these two organizational engines (the board and the staff) together

But this chapter isn't called "Leadership: The Happy Place"; it's about transitions. So let's get to it. Let's talk about how to get the wrong people off the bus and what to do when the right people opt out. The following profiles are amalgams of real attributes I have seen in problematic board chairs.

The AUTOCRAT

Symptoms

This board chair has appeal to board members who are on the board just so they can say they are. This board chair gets it done and tells people what to do. Power is a significant perk of this gig for the Autocrat. Board meetings are ridiculously efficient, so much so that board members wondered why they had to show up at all. Then there is the executive director. He feels micromanaged. Board meeting agendas are set by the chair with little input from anyone. The Autocrat will have definite opinions about staff performance and won't hesitate to tell you so, sometimes directing you to take action. At raise time, the Autocrat may be the board chair who believes that nonprofit folks somehow deserve to be paid less. And he might not be a big champion of overhead expenses. Oh, and he will want to review many things that get sent out to stakeholders. He will also be the first to find typos in your annual report before saying a single good word about the extraordinary work.

Challenges

- Strong board members who came to have a voice, add value to strategic discussions, and ask tough questions will feel stifled. They will be serious flight risks. Weak board members will just like that stuff is being taken care of.
- Miserable staff leader. The Autocrat is tough and intimidating so there is no release valve for sharing feedback with anyone about the challenges the Autocrat is creating. Staff leader is disempowered and feels a lack of trust. Staff leader becomes a flight risk.

Antidote

- Change rests in the hands of those strong and disgruntled board members. If you see yourself in this scenario, please know two things. First if *you* are disgruntled, you can bet your E.D. is feeling even worse. And disgruntled, unmotivated E.D.s don't typically do their best work.
- Please do not jump ship. You came to be a strong and engaged board member, so here's your chance. It just isn't the kind of strength you anticipated. Find one or two other board members who feel similarly and do three things:
  1. Take the E.D. out to lunch. Share some of the challenges you see at the board level with the Autocrat's leadership and see if you can get her to talk about her own concerns. Just that outreach alone will give the E.D. hope. Strategize together

on how things can be different. And ask the E.D. to be patient. Change may not happen quickly but, together, perhaps you can develop a plan. You will all have ideas.

2. Perhaps you, as a board member, are not chairing a committee and maybe you should. What about joining the executive committee where you can start to ask questions in a smaller setting with the E.D. present. Maybe it's time for a few of you to recommend agenda items for the upcoming board meeting.

3. Begin to make the Autocrat feel just a bit uncomfortable. It is possible that the Autocrat will thaw a bit—maybe he thought he was the only one who was willing to do things. Or maybe not. Maybe he will just get angry. To this I say: So what? Because if you sit idly by and lose a five-star staff leader, that will cause a great deal more upheaval in your organization than a bad temper from an Autocrat. Here's the deal: You joined the board because of your deep sense of responsibility. Time to put it to good use. Be part of the solution.

BOARD CHAIR ON STEROIDS

This is different from a five-star board chair. As I mentioned in an early chapter, a five-star board member is a leader, a mentor, a facilitator. He is someone who builds a strong team of board members, each given the opportunity to lead and contribute.

Symptoms

This board chair (Steroids) always feels it's just easier to do it herself. If she does ask a board member to draft something or create a plan, she'll spend hours rewriting something that was 85 percent there to make it, in her mind, an A+. In so doing, her fellow board member feels undermined and wonders why he bothered.

This happens with the executive director as well. But the E.D. knows how hard Steroids works and so what if the high performance of the board rests largely on one person's shoulders. As long as the board is doing its thing, the E.D. won't worry that others are disengaged or M.I.A.

Challenge

The board leadership pipeline is dormant. No one steps up because no one needs to. Executive director will likely be very frustrated but much less of a flight risk. The board *is* delivering for the organization—through the Steroids approach of a single individual. The biggest challenge in this scenario, as I mentioned earlier, is that the board chair job looks absolutely impossible and so replacing Steroids is going to be really tough.

Antidote

Very similar to the Autocrat antidote but easier. The power dynamic is part of Steroid's hardwiring, but not in a dysfunctional way, and so the approach can be more positive and collaborative as strong board members can actually *discuss* a higher level of engagement. And, typically, Steroids wants what is best for the organization and will, upon reflection and with discussion, understand that the chair job must seem doable for someone who can't toss 150 percent of their time at the organization but can still be a first-rate board leader to step up.

THE WEAKEST LINK

Walk into a boardroom with a meeting run by the weakest link and here's the first thing you will notice. You will have absolutely no idea who the board chair is.

Symptoms

Board meetings are poorly run. "Link" is typically insecure, passive, and not very strategic. The biggest personalities and loudest voices rule the day. Link will allow a board discussion to go on forever and right into the weeds.

Challenges

This board chair drives the board crazy. Almost all the other board members know they could do a better job leading the board but doing so would mean they would have to raise their hands. Link was typically either the lone volunteer or the only one who could be persuaded. Board members are not pushed to do their best. And neither is the executive director. The E.D. does not have the strategic thought partner she or he needs. Link doesn't ask good questions, lets the E.D. totally run the show (which is fine if the E.D. is a rock star but a massive liability if the E.D.'s performance is a problem). Link does not anticipate problems or anticipate what the board might need to know. Typically, a strong E.D. will actually find Link appealing *(Link leaves me alone so I can do my job without interference from a board that is not helping me anyway)*. Your big risk here is not that your E.D. will scram. Instead, your risk is that you lose the checks and balances that an effective board chair provides. A weak board chair can lead to a weak and ineffective board. It puts the organization in a very vulnerable position for the board not to take its responsibility to provide strong oversight seriously. This profile may in fact be the scariest.

> Almost all the other board members know they could do a better job leading the board but doing so would mean they would have to raise their hands.

Antidote

As board members, you actually voted for Link! Maybe you didn't realize Link would be so weak? I'm not buying it. People don't change their stripes that easily. Tell the truth. The board needed a chair and you weren't willing. Or you didn't work to persuade someone to do it and offer your own leadership on a committee as support. And so inaction leads to the election of Link. She or he couldn't do much harm, right?

Wrong.

Link must be supported, and quickly. And, of course, the board needs to find a strong replacement to stand in the wings. A group of like-minded board members needs to talk and figure out how to reduce the liability of the chair. This group, whether it is formally created like the executive committee or informally created, understands that the board needs leadership and Link isn't the one to provide it. It must also be accompanied by the understanding of and a commitment to building board leadership to ensure that folks like Link do not ever find their way onto the board chair ballot.

Okay, so staff leaders, do you feel wildly validated? Hang on. Because now it's your turn.

STAFF LEADERS WHO AREN'T LEADING

Hiring an executive director is the most important decision a board of directors makes. It's also time consuming. Really time consuming. And when a group of volunteers makes this kind of investment followed by a big decision, they are very invested in the successful

> Hiring an executive director is the most important decision a Board of Directors makes.

outcome of that decision. Sometimes overly invested.

> Dear Joan,
> I'm really torn. Three months ago, we hired a new executive director. I was the candidate's biggest advocate. Yes, the vote went in his favor but it was not unanimous. As the board chair, I have been managing and providing oversight and there have been signs from Day One that our new E.D. has challenges. Even staff has been sending cryptic signals to me that point to trouble. We were told he was strong in finance but now I've heard he barely knows Excel. We have the budget for him to hire an assistant and I think that will help but he hasn't even started the process. His board report at his first board meeting made everyone very nervous—it was scattered and there was a lot of complaining and blaming about what he had not accomplished. He never developed a 90-day plan. And yet I find myself defending him. Am I just covering for him? Or justifying my own advocacy for his hiring? One day I feel like he needs to go and the next I feel like he just needs more resources.
> Signed,
> On the Fence

Dear Fence,

Based on the little I have to go on here, you should come down off the fence. This E.D. has got to go and you need to let go of your personal investment in his hire. There is something way bigger at stake here than your ego. Yes, the organization's reputation will take a hit, but it should. Sounds like, for whatever reason, you made a hiring mistake.

THE FIVE-ALARM BLAZE

Symptoms

See the preceding *Dear Joan* letter. And, by the way, the board chair in the preceding letter probably knows only half of it. When you make a hiring mistake, the problems begin to surface in all sorts of ways. You start to see smoke. Maybe even a few licks of flames. Trust me, there is more where that came from. But here are a few 90-day markers.

- Does she know the finances of your organization cold?
- Has she made a direct solicitation for a donation from an individual?
- Has she met with the 25 most important stakeholders in the organization to introduce herself to and share her vision?
- Does she have a really good read on staff?
- At her first board meeting, did she present a 90-day plan?
- Has she been in regular communication with the board, biweekly emails, for example, to share successes and updates and to enlist board support in specific ways?

If the answers to most of these questions is "no," I would suggest that "Blaze" is in the house.

Challenges

I have no interest in insulting your intelligence, so I won't list all the reasons that Blaze can hurt your organization, but there's something important to say. Problems are usually clear in the first 30 days. I will spend an hour on the phone with a prospective client who is seeking coaching as a new E.D. In that hour, I can tell. I can tell if you have a potential star or a potential Blaze. It has to do with tone, with authenticity, with the clarity of purpose I hear in the voice and in what they say. Board members see it, too, if they allow themselves to do so. Because of the investment of time and energy in the hire, the board will be reluctant to move decisively when it is clear that the fire is a-burning. I say

> Problems are usually clear in the first 30 days.

this with respect and admiration, but you are almost not to be trusted to evaluate.

The idea that you made a mistake will feel awful and fearful. The fear is the worst part. You fear that your credibility as a board will be greatly damaged with a failed hire and that, as a result, the credibility of the organization and its work will be diminished in the eyes of those you serve and those who fund you.

You and your Type A board members will come up with a hundred justifications. You'll supervise more closely. You'll provide scaffolding—maybe a coach. You see some signs of turnaround; or at least they will feel like signs. This happens because you want to see them so badly and because another search feels so overwhelming. Maybe you can make this work.

Can I let you in on another secret I think board members don't know? From the outside looking in, the board takes a bigger credibility hit when it waits. Donors meet with the E.D. and wonder if the board gets it. Colleagues in your sector will meet him and wonder if the board gets it. And the longer you wait, the less your stakeholders will believe that you get it. And that's the biggest problem of all to the credibility of the board and your organization—that stakeholders believe that the board doesn't see what is so obvious to them.

Antidote

Board members should fan out and casually connect with varying stakeholders as soon as something just doesn't feel right. Do this as a stewardship effort (this is important with anyone you hire). It's time for reconnaissance and external validation.

Next, in that first meeting with the new E.D. and the chair, ask the E.D. how she intends to tackle the first 90 days. You should receive a thoughtful answer, you should be asked for input and you should be told that you are going to get something in writing for the two of you to review together. If this does not happen, then ask for one. Use this deliverable as a way to assess who you have in the driver's seat.

Next, be sure the board is holding tight to the reins of board recruitment. Please! If this new E.D. builds the board the wrong way (and if he is a Five-Alarm Blaze, he might), he will pack it with allies. Allies who will vote in his favor on issues that matter. Oh, like voting to fire him, for example.

At the 90-day mark, the executive committee should go into executive session and have a candid conversation (yet another place that pro bono HR consultant could come in handy). I promise you that you will have more clues than you think you do—especially if you, as board members, do some stewardship of the stakeholders for feedback.

If you think this is a failed hire, create a plan to develop a paper trail. Put the E.D. on the equivalent of a performance improvement plan. If you have a real Blaze, she or he will not meet the goals you set in the plan. And then the process of cutting bait can begin.

One last piece of advice on this topic: Bring the search committee back together and appreciate the hell out of them. They will need moral support. They spent a ton of time on this and will feel like failures. And then, gently, ever so gently, begin a conversation about whether there were clues in the process. You need to learn so you get it right next time.

And then put this question out there. Did you have a very strong candidate pool or did you hire the best of a mediocre lot? This is the single biggest mistake search committees make. In the context of weak candidates, the person you hire may look quite good. And even the most wonderful search committee chair will feel internal and external pressure to make a recommendation to hire one of the mediocre lot. It is almost always a mistake. But volunteers can dedicate only so much time and they feel compelled to cross the finish line as quickly as possible. In this case, it's to the organization's detriment.

> Did you have a very strong candidate pool or did you hire the best of a mediocre lot?

TOAST

Trends illustrate that we are just entering a phase in which baby boomer executive directors are beginning to retire. Sometimes they are rock stars and you are devastated at the prospect of losing them. Sometimes they are no longer hitting on all their pistons. And sometimes it is just time for a new kind of leadership.

Symptoms

They haven't had a new, innovative idea in some time; they really don't have the energy to make needed changes (asking folks off the bus or bringing new folks onto the bus); and the organization becomes somewhat dormant. The board pushes for something new and keeps pushing. The resistance is either clear or passive. The organization is often still doing great work but the board finds itself seeing missed opportunities at every turn.

Challenges

They're obvious: frustrated board members—some who came with a lot of energy for innovation move on. Someone running out the clock is not pushing hard enough. And sometimes, the E. D. with the long tenure is not savvy in social marketing and digital engagement and does not see it as a priority.

Antidote

One answer is, of course, to wait it out. The work continues to be of high quality. And yet there is a growing recognition that your clients and donors deserve more. Another option is to push harder for change, turning the heat up and sending messages of all sorts that more is expected. The E.D. might accelerate a departure timetable. The third option is to work closely with the E.D. to create scenarios, projects, and initiatives that reenergize the leader. I have seen highly innovative, five-star leaders who have been in their jobs for years and when I ask the recipe, I will inevitably hear, *"I feel like my job is always different—I have had so many opportunities to reinvent myself."* If the E.D. is receptive, this can be an effective antidote.

THE FOUNDER (THE ONE WHO STICKS AROUND TOO LONG)

Now this is a very different kettle of fish from the other staff leader challenges. The symptoms and challenges are clear. The antidote requires the strongest board of all.

Symptoms

"Responsibility without authority" is the key symptom. Folks are given roles and responsibilities but decisions really rest with the founder. In addition, the board follows the founder rather than the other way around. The board is initially built with friends of the founder who do not rock the boat and sometimes are quite unclear about their own authority. Hiring practices are not formal and often folks hired are a degree or two of separation from the founder. Lastly, people come to work because of the cachet and charisma of the founder. For some, it wears off and there are others who become long-suffering number twos who work so hard to keep the team on track.

Challenges

There's a very long list here and it begins with staff attrition. Generally, those who found organizations (and this is true in the for-profit as well as the nonprofit sectors) are visionaries, leaders, the folks with the big ideas. They are infrequently the folks who can execute or manage. And processes like strategic planning feel cumbersome and limiting to the founder.

Antidote

The only antidote that I have ever seen work is the development of a strong board with new voices and faces that are not personally tied to the founder. If this board can begin to hold the founder accountable, there is hope. Money is another way to change the dynamic. If the organization is given a grant to do strategic planning and the board and staff are accountable to an external force (and one who is writing a big check), change is possible and the founder can be brought into alignment with the rest of the organization around a new road map.

But make no mistake, this is no easy feat. Sometimes the very best thing for the organization is to work with the founder to create some other kind of role that takes him out of the day-to-day operation of the organization (and *not on the board!*). This requires the board turning up the heat on the founder and then a great deal of diplomacy and finesse. It doesn't sound easy, does it? I'm not gonna lie; it's not. It's worth a shot if you believe in the mission of the organization and the sustainability of the organization with the founder in some lesser role.

Having done a deep dive into the profiles of leaders who present real challenges to your organization, shall we focus on another scenario—the leader you want to stay forever leaves *you*?

THE FIVE-STAR STAFF LEADER WHO CALLS IT QUITS

This is the scenario a board dreads. Early on in this person's tenure, you know you have struck gold. Have a glance back at Chapter 1 and review the superpowers of nonprofit leadership. You will see those superpowers in your leader. You hope it will last forever. And then it doesn't. It was a helluva ride but all good things . . .

As I mentioned, this is the one transition that rocks an organization to its core. The five-star leader is often beloved; his presence helps recruit staff and board members who want to be part of this winning team. This leader understands that it takes a village to build a five-star nonprofit—a strong board, the right staff, engaged volunteers, donors who are informed and appreciated, and a program strategy that is smart, impactful, and measurable. With this leader, everyone really does feel lucky to be a member of this village. I've seen it. It's kind of magical.

There are some ingredients to a smooth transition and let's take them one by one.

An E.D. Contract

Please tell me you were smart enough as an organization to offer your rock star a contract. And please tell me that it was a negotiation process that was fair and honored the contributions of your amazing leader, providing whatever incentives you could offer to ensure retention.

Let's say you didn't screw it up. In this contract, you have provided an incentive to your rock star to stay with you and work right up to the last day. Perhaps a month of salary for every year of service if they stay through the end of their contract (can you imagine working full throttle as an E.D. and shopping for a new gig? Me neither).

The contract should also include a date by which the E.D. is required to make her intentions known. I advise a six-month date before the end of the contract—at that date, the E.D. needs to let the board leadership know if she plans to engage in new contract negotiations.

I took my contract seriously and knew that six-month date cold. Being the planner that I am, my process began at the nine-month mark. I needed time and I did my due diligence. A big dose of soul searching and lots of conversation with my wife, and then with my five-star board chair, thought partner, and trusted friend.

I reached a decision not to renew based on three key reasons:

1. **Family Ties.** For me, it was about my family. It was a growing feeling of irresponsibility to my partner and our kids. Could I advocate for a cause and members of an entire marginalized community but not for my own kids as they traveled the turbulent waters of middle and high school? This increasing

feeling of shirking my responsibilities was impossible for me to ignore.

2. **The Future Was Down the Hall.** I'm not saying that I groomed a successor who took over for me when I left because an external candidate replaced me. I mean something else.

I remember the meeting so vividly. As I was deciding, my lead program person asked me to meet someone she thought was a rock star candidate for an open position on her team. The two of them sat in my office and we talked. He was a rock star. So was she. (Note: Now they are both successful and innovative five-star E.D.s at organizations that are so very lucky to have them.) The conversation was engaging and I learned a lot from both of them. And, in that moment, it was clear that I was staring at the future and that, not only *could* I pass the baton with confidence, but I saw that I *should*.

3. **No Unfinished Business.** I did what I set out to do. I rebuilt an organization and developed programs and campaigns with real and substantive impact. And I believed two things: (1) a fresh set of eyes is very good for an organization, and (2) the future strategy of GLAAD's work might best be shaped and executed by someone more savvy about the future of the media business.

There is one last question that it is really important to ask yourself: Are you staying because you have no picture of what is next? Maybe my own career path enabled me to be more imaginative. Every new role I stepped into, including nonprofit leadership, enriched me, challenged me, played to my strengths, and pushed me to address some of my vulnerabilities. I knew I was heading to New Jersey to be a stay-at-home mom but I was making a growing list of adventures I could embark on while still ensuring that our high school kids did not come home to an empty house. One of these

> Are you staying because you have no picture of what is next?

adventures was starting a nonprofit consulting practice and then ultimately a blog, a podcast, and the book you are now holding in your hands. I'd say it worked out mighty well.

But that was me. Others find themselves paralyzed. It is a very bad reason to stay and I always encourage these folks to seek outside support as they grapple with the next chapter of their lives.

The single biggest support in helping me think through the decision was my board chair. I let her in on my thinking before the six-month deadline. She was smart, strategic, and had become a trusted friend. Once my decision was clear, we knew that how it was communicated, to whom, and when, were critical pieces of the puzzle. And so, Karen, the board chair, with a bit of help from my assistant (I called him Radar O'Reilly because anticipating was his superpower) developed a full plan. From soup to nuts. It included a timetable. Who would find out when and in what order. What were my talking points? What were the organization's talking points? I drafted a letter to go to the GLAAD stakeholders. I used a trusted friend with a public relations background to draft a great press release. We developed Q and A for the press. I persuaded my board chair to solicit a proposal from a transition consultant firm to help board leadership get the transition right, internally and externally.

As the governing body, board members were informed first, a week before our January 2005 board meeting. These were board members all over the country, so I stayed home and made the calls one by one using the talking points and laid out the communications plan and the order of notifications. They were sad but so much calmer for all the planning. I demanded their confidentiality until the staff had been told. Once told, the board chair sent out a revised board agenda that included a presentation from the transition firm.

Once the board had all been notified, I had a highly orchestrated internal and then external communications plan. I had my talking points ready and the board had okayed my letter to stakeholders and the press release. After the staff, there was a long list of donors, volunteers, community leaders, people of influence, journalists, and former staff. Radar O'Reilly brought me a new cup of coffee before my current one was empty as I made call after call. I talked in real time to many, left messages if I had to, and then at the appointed time, we hit "send" on the stakeholder letter and the press release.

When I tell folks this story, they suggest that I may have some OCD going on. It is possible, but it is clear to me that handling this process with this kind of attention to detail is important and sends a very strong message to the community you represent and the stakeholders who stand by you.

It bears repeating. Leadership transitions—whether someone chooses to step off the bus and on to a new adventure or you recognize that your constituents need and deserve leadership they are not getting—are one of the top most destabilizing events in a nonprofit's trajectory. And demanding the best at the staff and board level, making tough decisions when you have to and managing the departures of those you wish would stay—these are as important a set of jobs as any nonprofit board does.

And your organization will be judged as much by the "how" (the process and communication) as it will be by who fills the shoes.

Folks pay a lot of attention. Because for those who care deeply about your mission, there is so much riding on the choices you make and how you make them.

THE ON-DECK CIRCLE

Building the Farm Team

If you have ever served on a board, there has been that executive session once a year without staff that focuses on this topic. And the topic is always described just this bluntly: *"We need to talk about what happens if Joan gets hit by a bus."*

> We need to talk about what happens if Joan gets hit by a bus.

Not only is it deeply offensive to anyone who has experienced the unimaginable loss of a friend or family member this way, but it also ends up being this conversation you have so you can say that you have had it. I have never found them to be helpful. Not long ago, I finally figured out why.

Boards are not only asking the wrong question, but going about it all wrong. Of course, they mean well. The topic, however you slice and dice it, is about the board's duty to consider succession planning. The problem is that the topic gets discussed through the lens of crisis.

> The problem is that the topic gets discussed through the lens of crisis.

At the risk of alienating Mets fans, I am an unabashed New York Yankees fan. I went to school in the Bronx and cut just a few classes in the spring before finals to head to the stadium.

Now, you don't have to be a baseball fan to appreciate the accomplishments of someone like Yankee shortstop Derek Jeter, who retired in 2014. The management couldn't wait until Jeter made his announcement; they needed to plan and be ready. The organization scouted and identified a replacement well before Jeter made it official. It's time for nonprofits to think in this vein.

Rather than framing succession planning through a crisis lens, organizations need to talk regularly with the E.D. (in executive session). Who are the rock stars? Possible successors? Are they folks that, with professional development, can grow into a more senior spot?

Why isn't *that* the conversation the board is having with the E. D.? Tell us about your staff. How do we retain the rock stars? What skills and attributes can we build that could turn them into organizational leadership material? Should we invest in a coach for her?

It's time for nonprofits to take a different approach to succession planning. Create an intentional process and please don't treat it like crisis management. Build a farm team of board and staff, recruit folks with potential, and groom them. Give them leadership opportunities and evaluate them.

Of all the antidotes included here about stability during transition, this may be the most important one of all. Build a stable, effective organization with great people and I guarantee you the transition will be stable too. And your communities and donors will appreciate and respect you for maintaining stability where others simply cannot.

> Build a stable, effective organization with great people and I guarantee you the transition will be stable too.

"I'm feeling in control, powerful, and so lucky to have this job. Do you think that's a side effect of the new meds?"

Chapter 9 You Are the Champions

I know who you are. I write to you and for you every week. You have been clients. You have been board colleagues of mine. You have been fellow staff leaders. You have been board members I worked to recruit. You educate our young people, you deliver meals, you work to cure illnesses and fight the stigma often associated with them. You fight for equality for women, people of color and LGBT folks. You provide beds to the homeless, put battered women back on their feet. You are storytellers who do not allow us to forget. You protect our lands, you navigate a complex world for those who are new here. You remind society of the power of religion and remind us of the power of deep faith. You bring music, theatre, and dance to us and in so doing, make us think, feel, and lift us up.

Yes, that's it. You lift us up. Each and every one of you. And you stand shoulder to shoulder with 11 million colleagues who head to work at a nonprofit every day, each of you doing your part to repair the world. You also stand shoulder to shoulder with over 60 million people who give of their time to causes they care about. Studies tell us that roughly 25 percent of Americans engage in some kind of volunteer work.

It's quite a big tribe. I like the word *tribe*. I wish more staff and board leaders felt that sense of tribe. So often I hear leaders talk about being overwhelmed and feeling alone.

You are hardly alone. You are in the best of company. Noble company. And with every passing year, it feels like we need you more than ever. There is so much broken in our society and it gives me such hope knowing you are all out there—chipping away at the solutions that will lift us all up.

The work is hard. I know. I've been in the trenches. I've read hate mail. I've missed more than my share of school plays. I read it in the mail I receive and I see it in the eyes of my clients. Yes, optimism on one hand and on the other, stress, exhaustion. It feels like every decision matters. A *lot*. It feels like so much is riding on your ability to make an impact.

I spent two weeks at a health boot camp for people of a certain age. I learned so much about the value of taking good care of ourselves. I learned about the value of something else, too.

Interval training. You work hard—really hard. Then you take a short but real break. Then you repeat. I learned that this kind of training makes you stronger. Maybe you knew that but this was headline news to me.

The trajectory of some jobs looks like Figure 9.1. Peaks, lulls, plateaus.

And then there is the pace of the nonprofit world. *Everything* matters *all the time* (see Figure 9.2).

I wish someone had told me all this back in 1997—that I would never work so hard or care so much. That I would feel like I was letting the whole world down if I took a break. That interval training makes you stronger. That a "sprinter's pace" is

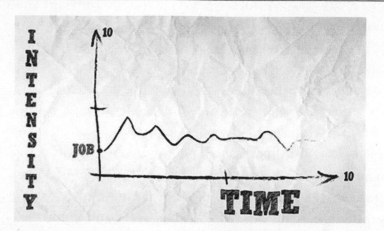

FIGURE 9.1   A simple and easy dashboard for the financially literate (and illiterate).

unsustainable and the issues the nonprofit sector addresses are of the "marathon" variety.

Maybe I wouldn't have almost killed my development director.

* * *

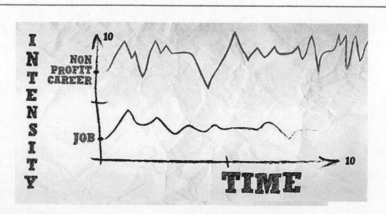

FIGURE 9.2   Why nonprofit leaders burn out.

And this, my fellow tribe members, is why I decided to write this book. Actually, it was more than a decision. I was *compelled*. Just as I am with each of my clients. I believe that this book can be of service to you.

Leading a nonprofit is tough and often thankless (and for board leaders, *unpaid, to boot)* and it is my fondest hope that this book offered you both philosophical and tactical takeaways that enable you to feel less alone and more effective.

In an effort to help the messy world of the nonprofit be just a bit tidier, here are some nice succinct sound bites worth keeping close to you as you continue to fight the good fight.

- A highly effective nonprofit is like a first rate twin-engine jet. Board and staff must work together in a model of shared leadership and partnership. Alone, neither is able to manage, plan, and grow resources in the passionate pursuit of your mission.
- Your power as a leader comes from all around you. It takes a village to run a five-star nonprofit. Clients, donors, volunteers—a diverse group of people with value to add must be engaged. You are not alone. Look around you. And look to Kermit the Frog as inspiration.
- Learn to tell a helluva story about your work. There are fewer elements of the human culture that are more primitive than the narrative. And while talking about your organization should be one of the easiest things in the world for you to do, it turns out it is mighty tough. Practice, get it right, and get people at "hello."
- Take time to ask the tough questions. If the words *strategic planning* lead you to break out in a rash, don't use them. Dedicate time instead with your "village" to pose the tough strategic questions you must answer in order to create the most expedient and effective road to the fulfillment of your mission.
- Your love for your organization and its work must trump your fear of asking. No color commentary needed here.

• Manage people in 3-D. Take the time to know and understand your fellow board members, your staff, and those closest to the organization. Ask them to tell you why this work matters. Give them a voice. Trust me. It will inspire *you* when your people bring *all* of themselves to the work.

• Anticipate. Remember my comment about interval training? The break doesn't have to be a walk around the block or a long weekend. It can also mean a break from your role as firefighter to allow for *planning*. This kind of break will make you stronger for sure and will enable you to weather the storms that will surely come your way.

• Take a firm and compassionate hold on the organization during a transition. A change in leadership is more destabilizing than you know, especially on the staff side. Take this transition seriously and be sure your board is as strong and effective as it can possibly be to recruit the best leaders and retain them as well as your star staff for the long haul.

One last thing.

It is a privilege to have a leadership role in a nonprofit. It is a joy to have the opportunity to dedicate your skills, life experience, time, energy, and passion to a cause you care deeply about.

That said, the work is tough and often thankless. And so I will end with just two words:

Thank you.

Bibliography

CHAPTER 2: YOU'VE GOT TO GET ME AT HELLO

Collins, Jim. *From Good to Great in the Social Sector*. New York: HarperCollins, 2005.

Hesselbein, Frances. *Hesselbein on Leadership*. San Francisco: Jossey-Bass, 2002.

"Make-A-Wish America: Our Mission." *Make-A-Wish America*. October 24, 2016. http://wish.org/about-us/our-story/our-mission.

CHAPTER 3: CO-PILOTS IN A TWIN-ENGINE PLANE

Heath, Chip, and Dan Heath. *Made to Stick: Why Some Ideas Survive and Others Die*. New York: Random House, 2007.

Steinbeck, John. *East of Eden*. New York: Penguin, 2002.

CHAPTER 4: THE KEY IS NOT IN THE ANSWERS. IT'S IN THE QUESTIONS

E. T., The Extra-Terrestrial. Swank, 1982.

CHAPTER 5: YOU CAN DO THIS

Dwight D. Eisenhower. "Remarks at the National Defense Executive Reserve Conference," November 14, 1957. Online by Gerhard Peters and John T. Woolley, *The American Presidency Project*. www .presidency.ucsb.edu/ws/?pid=10951.

Kruse, Kevin. *"Stephen Covey: 10 Quotes That Can Change Your Life." Forbes* magazine, July 16, 2012. www.forbes.com/sites/kevinkruse/ 2012/07/16/the-7-habits/#79870e562705.

O'Donovan, Dana, and Noah Rimland Flower. "The Strategic Plan Is Dead. Long Live Strategy. (SSIR)." *Stanford Social Innovation Review,* January 10, 2013. https://ssir.org/articles/entry/the_strategic_plan_is_ dead._long_live_strategy.

CHAPTER 7: WHEN IT HITS THE FAN

Bonk, Kathy, and Emily Tynes. *Strategic Communications for Nonprofits.* San Francisco: Jossey Bass, 2008.

Fearn-Banks, Kathleen. *Crisis Communications: A Casebook Approach.* 4th edition. Mahwah, NJ: Erlbaum, 2011.

Fink, Steven. *Crisis Communications: The Definitive Guide to Managing The Message.* New York: McGraw-Hill, 2013 (138–179).

Hamblin, James. "The Physiological Power of Altruism." *The Atlantic,* December 30, 2015. www.theatlantic.com/health/archive/2015/12/ altruism-for-a-better-body/422280/.

Pink, Daniel. "The Puzzle of Motivation." *Dan Pink: TED Talk,* July 2009. https://www.ted.com/talks/dan_pink_on_motivation?language=en.

Sinek, Simon. *Start with Why: How Great Leaders Inspire Everyone to Take Action.* New York: Portfolio, 2009.

CHAPTER 8: HELLO, I MUST BE GOING

Associated Press. "Greenpeace Loses $5.2 Million on Currency Trading."
    USA Today, June 16, 2014. www.usatoday.com/story/news/nation/
    2014/06/16/greenpeace-loses-millions/10568731/

"Crisis Intel and Reports." Institute for Crisis Management, October 25,
    2016. http://crisisconsultant.com/crisis-intel-reports/.

Drape, Joe. "Sandusky Guilty of Sexual Abuse of 10 Young Boys." *New
    York Times,* June 23, 2012: A1.

Goodman, J. David. "DNA Confirms Body Parts Belong to Missing Boy
    with Autism." *New York Times,* January 22, 2014: A16.

"Orlando Shooting." *New York Times*, June 20, 2016. www.nytimes
    .com/news-event/2016-orlando-shooting.

Yardley, Jim. "Tower of Logs Collapses at Texas A&M, Killing 11." *New
    York Times*, November 18, 1999. www.nytimes.com/1999/11/19/us/
    tower-of-logs-collapses-at-texas-a-m-killing-11.html.

Index